Diseases and Disorders

Leukemia

Titles in the Diseases and Disorders series include:

Diseases and Disorders

Leukemia

by Melissa Abramovitz

LUCENT BOOKS
SAN DIEGO, CALIFORNIA

THOMSON
─────✳───── ™
GALE

Detroit • New York • San Diego • San Francisco
Boston • New Haven, Conn. • Waterville, Maine
London • Munich

616.994
ABR

Library of Congress Cataloging-in-Publication Data

Abramovitz, Melissa, 1954–
    Leukemia / by Melissa Abramovitz.
        p. cm. — (Diseases and disorders series)
Includes bibliographical references and index.
    Summary: Discusses leukemia, its causes, diagnosis, and treatment, living with the disease, and current trends in research and medication.
    ISBN 1-56006-863-9 (hbk. : alk.paper)
    1. Leukemia—Juvenile literature. [1. Leukemia. 2. Diseases.] I. Title. II. Series.
    RC643 .A274 2003
    616.99'419—dc21

                                                                2002003668

Copyright © 2003 by Lucent Books,
an imprint of The Gale Group
10911 Technology Place, San Diego, CA 92127
Printed in the U.S.A.

Table of Contents

"The Most Difficult Puzzles Ever Devised"

CHARLES BEST, ONE of the pioneers in the search for a cure for diabetes, once explained what it is about medical research that intrigued him so. "It's not just the gratification of knowing one is helping people," he confided, "although that probably is a more heroic and selfless motivation. Those feelings may enter in, but truly, what I find best is the feeling of going toe to toe with nature, of trying to solve the most difficult puzzles ever devised. The answers are there somewhere, those keys that will solve the puzzle and make the patient well. But how will those keys be found?"

Since the dawn of civilization, nothing has so puzzled people—and often frightened them, as well—as the onset of illness in a body or mind that had seemed healthy before. A seizure, the inability of a heart to pump, the sudden deterioration of muscle tone in a small child—being unable to reverse such conditions or even to understand why they occur was unspeakably frustrating to healers. Even before there were names for such conditions, even before they were understood at all, each was a reminder of how complex the human body was, and how vulnerable.

While our grappling with understanding diseases has been frustrating at times, it has also provided some of humankind's most heroic accomplishments. Alexander Fleming's accidental discovery in 1928 of a mold that could be turned into penicillin has resulted in the saving of untold millions of lives. The isolation of the enzyme insulin has reversed what was once a death sentence for anyone with diabetes. There have been great strides in combating conditions for which there is not yet a cure, too. Medicines can help AIDS patients live longer, diagnostic tools such as mammography and ultrasounds can help doctors find tumors while they are treatable, and laser surgery techniques have made the most intricate, minute operations routine.

This "toe-to-toe" competition with diseases and disorders is even more remarkable when seen in a historical continuum. An astonishing amount of progress has been made in a very short time. Just two hundred years ago, the existence of germs as a cause of some diseases was unknown. In fact, it was less than 150 years ago that a British surgeon named Joseph Lister had difficulty persuading his fellow doctors that washing their hands before delivering a baby might increase the chances of a healthy delivery (especially if they had just attended to a diseased patient)!

Each book in Lucent's *Diseases and Disorders* series explores a disease or disorder and the knowledge that has been accumulated (or discarded) by doctors through the years. Each book also examines the tools used for pinpointing a diagnosis, as well as the various means that are used to treat or cure a disease. Finally, new ideas are presented—techniques or medicines that may be on the horizon.

Frustration and disappointment are still part of medicine, for not every disease or condition can be cured or prevented. But the limitations of knowledge are being pushed outward constantly; the "most difficult puzzles ever devised" are finding challengers every day.

A Dreaded and Frightening Disease

THE WORD *LEUKEMIA* strikes terror into the hearts and minds of those who encounter it. Beverly, a mother whose little boy developed the disease, remembers the panic and shock she felt on hearing the diagnosis: "I felt like a bomb had exploded in me. I had so many complicated feelings, and I was very scared."[1]

One of the main reasons leukemia frightens people so much is that it is a form of cancer that takes many lives and causes incalculable suffering despite dramatic advances in medical science over the past several decades. "Cancer is a word that disturbs us. It carries an image of a deadly invader; it is chilling because it can mean a death sentence,"[2] notes Dr. S.K. Kaura in *A Family Doctor's Guide to Understanding and Preventing Cancer*.

Leukemia, though, carries more terror than most cancers because it is the most common cancer among children. Each year, over thirty-five hundred children in the United States alone are diagnosed with this deadly disease, and it is considered to be one of the leading causes of death among children under age fifteen.

Leukemia also affects many adults; the Leukemia and Lymphoma Society estimates that there are over thirty thousand new cases and twenty thousand deaths each year in the United States. For unknown reasons, the disease strikes more Caucasians and fewer Chinese, Japanese, and Koreans than people of other ethnic backgrounds, and in addition affects more males than females. About 56 percent of leukemia victims are boys and men.

Anyone, Anytime, Anyplace

Even armed with these types of statistics, doctors say the scariest part about this form of cancer is that it is virtually impossible to predict who will get it. Leukemia can attack healthy individuals with frightening suddenness and speed, as twelve-year-old Marquita discovered: "When the doctor called my mom and told her he thought I had leukemia all I could do was cry . . . I never thought this could happen to me, but I found out that it could happen to anyone at any age,"[3] she said.

When a well-known sports figure, former Dallas Cowboys coach Tom Landry, received a diagnosis of leukemia at age seventy-four, the news was shocking and frightening for the general public as well as for Landry and his family. In an article in *Texas*

When Dallas Cowboys coach Tom Landry was diagnosed with leukemia, the public came to realize that the disease could strike anyone at any time.

Monthly magazine, writer Jim Atkinson spoke for many: "Some wondered how an old man could come down with a cancer widely thought to strike mostly children; others couldn't understand how someone who appeared to be so healthy could suddenly have a life-threatening condition."[4]

Hope Amid Terror

Despite leukemia's reputation as a merciless and unpredictable invader, modern medicine has made great progress in diagnosing, treating, and even curing the disease in many cases. As recently as forty years ago, some forms of leukemia were inevitably fatal within a few short weeks, but today the overall survival rate has tripled, making leukemia therapy one of the greatest success stories in the treatment of all types of cancer.

For children with the disease, the cure rate for the most common form of childhood leukemia is now close to 80 percent, so, especially for young people, getting leukemia is no longer an automatic death sentence. But the battle is far from over, for leukemia continues to take many lives, and treatment for the disease is painful, risky, and often leaves patients permanently impaired. Thus, doctors continue to search for more effective, less disabling methods of conquering leukemia in the hope that someday this dreaded cancer will no longer be a source of terror and suffering.

Chapter 1

What Is Leukemia?

L EUKEMIA IS A type of cancer that has afflicted people and animals for thousands of years. Anthropologists have discovered
evidence of the earliest known human case of the disease in a
skeleton found at Dakhla, an area of Egypt's western desert that
was a thriving political and economic center from 36 B.C. to A.D.
450. Scientists have determined that the skeletal remains contain
certain characteristic pits and holes unique to the bones of people with leukemia.

Other ancient evidence of leukemia comes from bone marrow
deoxyribonucleic acid (DNA) extracted from a fifteen-hundred-
year-old mummy found in the Atamaca Desert of Chile. Scientists discovered that the DNA contains a virus that is now known
to be associated with a type of leukemia called adult T-cell
leukemia. The researchers in this study have concluded that the
virus probably caused this type of leukemia in this ancient human as well.

When Was Leukemia First Identified?

Although it has existed throughout human history, leukemia was
not really understood as a distinct disease until doctors had the
tools to view the microscopic cells that make up living creatures.
While many forms of cancer consist of tumors that can be easily
seen or felt in specific areas of the body, leukemia affects the
blood and blood-forming tissues. It can only be detected using a
microscope and other tools that allow physicians to see or chemically test for its characteristics.

The great German pathologist Rudolf Virchow first identified
leukemia as a disease in 1845 after using a microscope to view

the blood of several patients with the same unexplained symptoms. Virchow noticed that the blood contained an overabundance of white blood cells and fewer than the normal amount of the other types of blood cells, so he named the disorder *weisses blut*, German for white blood. The English word *leukemia*, derived from the Greek terms *leukos*, meaning white, and *haima*, meaning blood, also refers to the preponderance of microscopic white blood cells. It should be noted that a leukemia patient's blood appears red when seen with the naked eye.

White Blood Cells

Since Virchow's time, doctors have come to understand a great deal more about the different types of cells involved in leukemia. Experts now define the disease as a cancer of the cells from which blood is formed. When these cells are prevented by the presence of leukemia from functioning normally, the most prominent result is the uncontrolled growth of white blood cells, also known as leukocytes.

Leukemia causes the uncontrolled growth of white blood cells, as shown in this microscopic view of bone marrow. The darkest areas are malignant leukocytes.

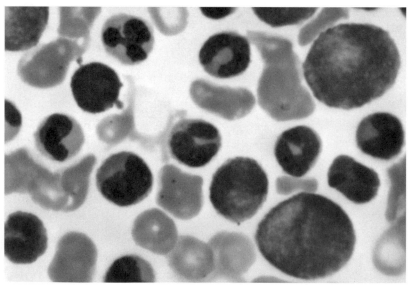

Leukocytes are mainly responsible for fighting infections such as viruses, bacteria, and fungi, along with combating other invaders like cancer cells. Each day the healthy human body produces about 10 billion new white blood cells, which generally live for one to two days.

There are three main kinds of leukocytes; all are important in understanding leukemia. Lymphocytes, the smallest white blood cells, are the major disease-fighting cells and come in three varieties called B cells, T cells, and NK cells. Bone marrow (B) and thymus (T) cells are the body's first line of response to contact with potentially dangerous substances known as antigens. B cells produce antibodies to attack these antigens, and T cells help the B cells begin their assault. Natural killer (NK) lymphocytes hunt down and kill cells infected by viruses or other foreign bodies like cancer cells.

Granulocytes and monocytes, the other major types of white blood cells, surround, engulf, and poison foreign invaders with powerful chemicals. Some granulocytes are responsible for releasing poisons to neutralize specific antigens. Other granulocytes release chemicals known as histamines; these chemicals trigger an allergic response to an invader. Monocytes, the largest type of leukocyte, are particularly effective against antigens like fungi and certain bacteria not killed by granulocytes. Monocytes also help remove dead bacteria and other foreign substances from body tissues.

Other Types of Blood Cells

Although leukemia primarily affects white blood cells, it also has an impact on the other kinds of blood cells—red blood cells and platelets. Red blood cells, also known as erythrocytes, mainly transport oxygen via hemoglobin, the substance that gives blood its red color. Platelets, or thrombocytes, are colorless blood cells that repair injured blood vessels and thus are essential for preventing life-threatening bleeding.

All types of blood cells—white, red, and platelets—originate in the bone marrow, a spongy tissue inside bone cavities. Marrow contains blood-forming stem cells, fat cells, and other cells which aid in the growth of blood cells. Stem cells start out with the potential to mature into any type of body cell. The stem cells found in the marrow are known as hematopoietic, or blood-forming stem cells; these stem cells have the potential to become any type of blood cell.

After being stimulated by certain hormones, stem cells in the marrow change into either myeloid- or lymphocyte-precursor cells. Myeloid-precursor cells normally mature into red blood cells, platelets, or monocyte and granulocyte white blood cells in the bone marrow. Lymphocyte-precursor cells mature into lymphocytes in the spleen, a fist-shaped organ important in fighting infections, or in the lymph system.

The lymph system is a circulatory system similar to the bloodstream except that it circulates a clear fluid called lymph instead of blood. Lymph mainly transports water, lymphocytes, and nutrients through channels that connect the lymph nodes, or groups of lymphocytes, and empties into the bloodstream through large ducts.

Life-Sustaining Blood and Lymph

The blood and lymph systems perform essential tasks that keep people alive, and diseases like leukemia that interfere with these functions can be deadly. In leukemia, any of the different kinds of white blood cells can become cancerous, and when this happens, these cells are prevented from maturing and performing their usual job of fighting infections. Unlike normal white blood cells, the cancerous leukocytes do not die within forty-eight hours, and this results in their buildup in the bone marrow and bloodstream.

Eventually, the buildup prevents stem cells in the marrow from maturing into red blood cells and platelets, so the leukemia patient begins to develop symptoms related to deficiencies in these cells too. The lack of red blood cells leads to anemia, a condition characterized by paleness, fatigue, and insufficient oxygen being transported throughout the body. The presence of too few platelets results in bruising and bleeding. By the time such symptoms become obvious, leukemia victims

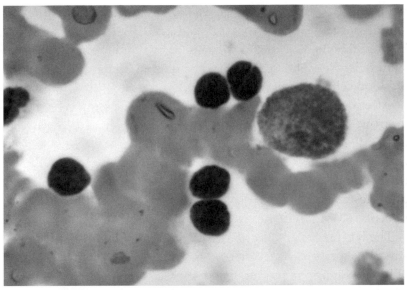

Leukemia in bone marrow. Since all blood cells originate in the bone marrow, the disease affects red blood cells and platelets as well as white blood cells.

or their families begin to suspect that something is terribly wrong. As the leukemia progresses further, the bone marrow becomes incapable of producing any normal blood cells and the vital organs cease to function at all.

Types of Leukemia

Leukemia takes different forms, which are classified according to the speed at which the disease proceeds and the particular white blood cells that become cancerous. Acute leukemias progress very rapidly, leading to death unless effective treatment is provided promptly. In acute leukemias, the bone marrow, lymph system, and bloodstream are overwhelmed by immature white blood cells known as blasts. The term *blast* can refer to any type of leukocyte that cancer prevents from maturing. Depending on the particular case, the development of these blasts may be arrested at various stages. Those cells that stop maturing at an early stage are entirely incapable of performing their designated functions. Sometimes blasts that stop maturing later on in their development cycle are able to carry out their jobs to a limited extent.

Chronic, or long-term, leukemias progress more slowly, so people with these forms of the disease tend to function better and for a longer period of time than do those with acute leukemias. The body continues to produce some normal blood cells and the person can often lead a fairly healthy life, sometimes for several years, until the normal cells are overwhelmed by the cancer cells. In contrast to the acute forms, many chronic cases involve an overabundance of mature white blood cells instead of or in addition to the immature blasts.

Besides classifying leukemia according to whether a particular case is acute or chronic, doctors also consider the kind of white blood cells that become cancerous. Lymphocytic leukemias involve lymphocytes—those leukocytes that normally mature in the spleen or lymph system—while myelogenous leukemias affect the granulocytes or monocytes that mature in the bone marrow. Specialists then designate a leukemia type as either acute or chronic lymphocytic or myelogenous; in addition they further break each type into subtypes depending on factors such as the involvement of T cells or B cells and the degree of maturity of any blast cells.

Acute Lymphocytic Leukemia

Acute lymphocytic leukemia (ALL) affects about 20 percent of adults and 80 percent of children with the disease. Since ALL is the most common form of leukemia among children, it is sometimes called childhood leukemia.

Most ALL cases, about 80 percent, involve B lymphocytes; this subtype is known as B-cell ALL. The rarer subtype that affects T cells is called T-cell ALL. Each subtype is broken down into further subtypes based on the shape, size, and degree of maturity of the leukemia cells.

In all the subtypes of ALL, some symptoms come from the production of huge numbers of immature blast cells, unable to function as true lymphocytes, which accumulate in the vital organs. Other symptoms are a result of these blasts preventing red blood cells and platelets from growing.

Symptoms of ALL may include flulike aches and fever, abnormal bruising, fatigue, paleness, night sweats, bleeding from the nose or mouth or in the eyes, enlarged lymph nodes, enlarged spleen or liver, abdominal tenderness, bone and joint pain, and frequent infections. Four-year-old Sabrina, for example, was tired, pale, running a fever, and had bruises all over her body when her parents took her to the doctor, and she was diagnosed with ALL. Without treatment, all the bleeding and infection would have killed the little girl within weeks.

Chronic Lymphocytic Leukemia

Chronic lymphocytic leukemia (CLL) strikes over eight thousand people in the United States each year. Most CLL patients are over age fifty, and men get this form of leukemia more than twice as often as women do.

Like ALL, CLL affects the lymphocytes, but with CLL the overabundant white cells mature and function normally, at least for a while. "Early in the disease, chronic lymphocytic leukemia may have little effect on a person's well-being. The disease may be discovered after finding an abnormal blood count during the course of a 'routine' medical examination or while the patient is under care for an unrelated condition,"[5] according to the Leukemia and Lymphoma Society. Eventually, however, the cancer prevents the lymphocytes from fully maturing and performing their necessary functions, resulting in what is called the accelerated phase of the disease. The accelerated phase may then progress to a so-called blast crisis, where immature, nonfunctioning lymphocytes overwhelm the patient.

One CLL patient felt fine and probably would not have found out about his condition until it entered the accelerated or blast-crisis stage had he not decided to become a blood donor. Tests at the blood bank, however, showed his blood contained an abnormally high number of leukocytes.

Other people with CLL have symptoms similar to those of ALL, but, rather than appearing all of a sudden, the CLL symptoms tend to develop gradually. The precise speed at which symptoms and the disease progress depends on the type of lymphocytes involved. The subtype B-CLL, affecting B lymphocytes, is the most common subtype, accounting for about 95 percent of CLL cases, and generally progresses more slowly than does T-CLL, the subtype affecting T lymphocytes. There are notable exceptions such as hairy cell leukemia, a subtype of B-CLL that is very aggressive and can be rapidly fatal. Hairy cell leukemia got its name because of the hairlike projections seen on the cancerous B cells under a microscope. It typically produces dramatic symptoms of a painfully enlarged spleen, frequent infections, weakness, fatigue, anemia, and bleeding due to a low platelet count.

T-CLL, usually the most aggressive CLL subtype, is also called adult T-cell leukemia, or ATL. Because it tends to affect the skin, nervous system, and lymph nodes, symptoms of ATL are likely to include skin rashes and infections, dizziness, seizures, and swollen lymph nodes.

Another subtype of CLL, known as prolymphocytic leukemia, can involve either B cells or T cells. Prolymphocytes are partly

A subtype of B-CLL known as hairy cell leukemia. The disease got its name from the hairlike projections seen on the cancerous B cells.

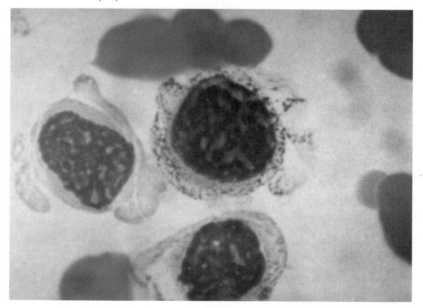

mature lymphocytes that may or may not be capable of fighting infections. The leukemia cells in this subtype are larger than those in the other forms of CLL.

Acute Myelogenous Leukemia

While ALL and CLL affect lymphocytes, the acute and chronic myelogenous forms of leukemia involve granulocytes or monocytes, the types of white blood cells that normally mature in the bone marrow. Acute myelogenous leukemia (AML) is the most common sort of leukemia in adults and affects about 20 percent of all children who have the disease.

AML is sometimes referred to as nonlymphocytic, monocytic, myelogenic, or myelocytic leukemia; all these terms signify its origins in the bone marrow rather than in the lymph system. This form of leukemia progresses very rapidly due to the production of large numbers of immature blast cells, which cannot perform their designated functions. The blasts also collect in the marrow and spleen, pushing aside and preventing normal blood cells from forming. In addition, they accumulate in vital organs such as the liver and impair the operation of these organs. Without treatment, AML is often fatal within a few weeks.

People with AML tend to display a wide variety of symptoms. In addition to the typical fatigue, fever, bruising, swollen lymph nodes and spleen, frequent infections, bone and joint pain, and bleeding seen in other types of leukemia, AML patients often have skin rashes, small red spots called petechiae, swollen gums, blurred vision or blindness, headaches, and seizures. One woman, for example, went to her doctor because of terribly swollen gums and mouth sores and discovered that she had a very aggressive type of AML.

Chronic Myelogenous Leukemia

Like AML, chronic myelogenous leukemia (CML) affects granulocytes or monocytes that mature in the bone marrow. Other names for CML are chronic myelocytic, chronic myeloid, and chronic granulocytic leukemia. Its chief characteristic is an overwhelming number of mature granulocytes and fewer immature blast cells in the early, or chronic, phase.

During the chronic phase, symptoms may be absent or develop gradually, often consisting of increasing fatigue, sweating, weight loss, and shortness of breath. Once the disease reaches the critical stage, known as the accelerated phase or blast crisis, usually within about five years, symptoms become dramatic and rapidly fatal if untreated. Accelerated-phase symptoms may include bleeding from a lack of platelets, infection due to white blood cells that no longer do their job, anemia that results from a lack of red blood cells, and abdominal pain from an enlarged spleen.

CML usually affects adults, but about 4 percent of childhood leukemia cases are of this type. It remains the only kind of leukemia not considered curable except with a bone marrow transplant.

How Are the Different Types of Leukemia Diagnosed?

Since people with leukemia of all types may have some, all, or none of the typical symptoms, diagnosing the disease and figuring out which subtype a patient has is often a difficult and lengthy process. To complicate the ordeal of classification and diagnosis, the disorder may first appear to be an altogether different disease.

Initially, a doctor may not think a patient with mild symptoms has anything seriously wrong. Tony, a young man in his twenties, for instance, visited his doctor after experiencing joint pain and bruising while playing rugby and was advised simply to take a pain medication. Only after Tony began having night sweats, extreme fatigue, and severe abdominal pain did the physician order blood tests, which revealed ALL.

According to leukemia survivor Barbara Lackritz, author of *Adult Leukemia*, sometimes a combination of a doctor's busy schedule and a patient's fear of making a big deal out of his or her symptoms can delay early diagnosis and lessen the chances of recovery or cure. "One problem that leukemia patients report is that some doctors do not take their concerns about unusual health phenomena seriously . . . such dismissal of the patient's

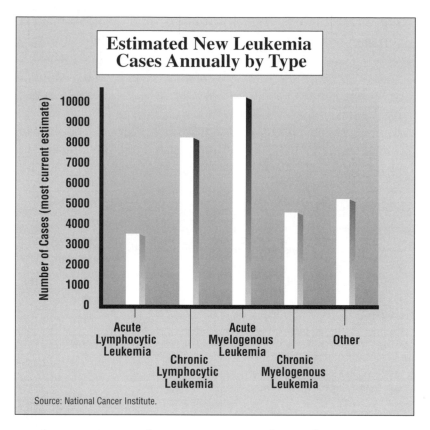

Estimated New Leukemia Cases Annually by Type

Source: National Cancer Institute.

concerns can cause the patient not to share what may be important diagnostic information,"[6] she notes. For this reason, leukemia experts emphasize the importance of reporting telltale signs and insisting on tests that can differentiate leukemia from other diseases like flu, mononucleosis, aplastic anemia, or cancers of the lymph system that share many of leukemia's symptoms.

Blood and Marrow Tests for Leukemia

Because of the variety of disorders that may be mistaken for leukemia, a reliable diagnosis can only be made using laboratory tests that examine blood and bone marrow under a microscope. A doctor will first order a complete blood count, or CBC, in which a small sample of the patient's blood is withdrawn and sent to a laboratory, where technicians count the total number of blood cells and check for abnormalities in the size and shape. The physician will also request a differential count, to determine the number of each type of blood cell.

The results of the CBC and differential tests can vary widely among different leukemia patients. Many patients have abnormally high numbers of certain types of white blood cells; for example, Mark, a CML patient, had a white cell count of 266,000 when he was diagnosed. A normal count is between 4,000 and 10,000. Other patients have fewer cells that appear abnormal since they are immature blasts. Still others have normal-appearing leukocytes that keep dividing and refuse to die. Looking closely at these characteristics can give important clues as to whether the patient has acute or chronic leukemia and also whether lymphocytes or myelogenous cells are involved.

When a person's blood counts are abnormal, usually a doctor will refer the individual to a hematologist, who is a physician

Doctors must analyze a sample of a patient's blood in order to diagnose leukemia. They count the different types of blood cells and check for abnormalities in size and shape.

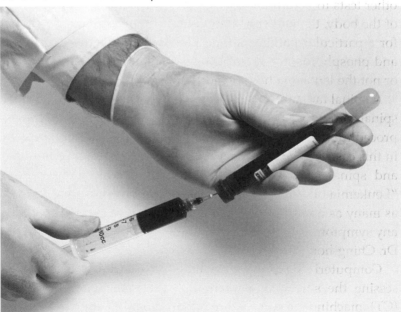

specializing in blood diseases, or to an oncologist, or cancer specialist. The specialist will then order more tests such as bone marrow sampling to find out what kind of blood cells in the marrow are affected. Since some subtypes of leukemia like hairy cell leukemia and adult forms of myelogenous leukemia may not show any cancer cells in the bloodstream, a bone marrow sample may also be the only reliable method of diagnosing these subtypes.

A doctor obtains a bone marrow sample by means of a bone marrow aspiration or a bone marrow biopsy. In an aspiration, the physician inserts a long, narrow needle into the patient's hip or breastbone, withdraws a small sample of marrow cells, and prepares the sample for examination under a microscope. In a biopsy, a needle with a wider opening is used to remove a tiny chunk of bone with the marrow attached. Patients report that these procedures are extremely painful, even with sedation.

Tests to Detect the Spread of Leukemia

Besides looking at the blood and marrow for leukemia cells, a doctor specializing in blood disorders or cancer will also perform other tests to determine the extent of the cancer in various parts of the body, the leukemia subtype, and the best course of action for a particular patient. A blood test for the chemicals uric acid and phosphorus, for example, is often done to find out whether or not the leukemia has spread to the kidneys and other organs.

A spinal tap, where cerebrospinal fluid is withdrawn from the spinal cord with a needle, is an extremely delicate, painful biopsy procedure that can indicate whether the leukemia has spread— in this case to the central nervous system consisting of the brain and spinal cord, where it can trigger deadly complications. "Leukemia blast cells can be seen in CSF (cerebrospinal fluid) in as many as a third of ALL patients, most of whom will not have any symptoms of disease in the brain,"[7] explains leukemia expert Dr. Ching-hon Pui.

Computerized scanning machines offer additional ways of assessing the spread of leukemia. A computerized tomography (CT) machine produces three-dimensional X-ray images that

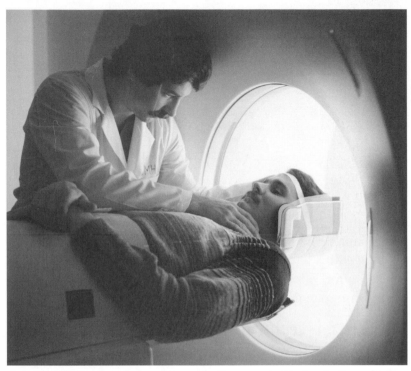

A patient undergoes a CT scan to assess the spread of leukemia throughout his body.

help doctors spot organ damage from leukemia cells. In another diagnostic method, the patient is injected with a solution containing radioactive particles of the chemical element gallium. Since cancer cells tend to absorb gallium more readily than normal cells do, they light up when the patient's body is viewed under a machine known as a gallium scanner.

Tests for Genetic Abnormalities

Other tests that help doctors correctly diagnose different types and subtypes of leukemia include sophisticated DNA tests for genetic abnormalities. Laboratory technicians use expensive, highly specialized equipment to identify chromosomes, the wormlike bodies that house genes in the cell center, or nucleus. These devices, called chromatographs, separate the tangled chromosome strands, arrange them on special paper, and photograph them. Then experts examine the photos, known as chromatograms, to see if there are mutations, or changes in the base chemicals that form the DNA strands. Certain mutations signify different types of leukemia; for instance, 90 percent of patients with CML have abnormalities known as the Philadelphia chromosome, so finding this feature during DNA testing is a good indication that a patient has CML.

Tests for Antigens and Antibodies

Other modern diagnostic techniques look not at genes, but at antigens and antibodies. Proteins such as these are found on the surface of leukemia cells and can help technicians identify the type of leukemia present. Cells that belong in the body carry molecules that act like a flag emblazoned with the words *belongs here*. Any substance without this flag will be recognized as an antigen and attacked by the immune system. One mechanism of attack involves B cells producing antibodies that go after a specific antigen. These antibodies then attach to the antigen by means of molecules that link up with molecules on the antigen—much like pieces of a puzzle fit together.

Tests with formidable names like immunophenotyping and flow cytometry can measure such antibody-antigen interactions and thereby reveal the precise proteins present in a blood or bone marrow sample. If the blood or marrow sample is exposed to a particular antibody stained with a fluorescent dye in the laboratory, the antibody will bind to an appropriate antigen if it is present in the sample, and the fluorescent dye will cause the cells with the antigen to light up when viewed with flow cytometry equipment. Since lymphocytic and myelogenous cells typically contain different types of antigens, measuring the number of such lit-up cells then enables a technician to identify the cells as either lymphocytic or myelogenous. The overall process of identifying cells by their surface antigens is known as immunophenotyping.

Knowledge about the antigens and antibodies is important not only for diagnosing a particular subtype of leukemia, but also for determining a prognosis, or expected outcome. The presence of certain antigen markers can give clues as to whether or not a patient has a good chance of recovery. The antigen known as CD10, for instance, is usually associated with a positive prognosis for ALL, while the antigen CD13 indicates the probability of a negative outcome in AML. By examining patterns of antigen markers, doctors can get a better idea of the exact nature and ideal course of action for an individual case of leukemia.

Staging the Disease

Armed with laboratory test results about the type, subtype, and extent of cancer spread, a physician must then determine the point to which a patient's disease has advanced. The labeling of the phase of a given patient's disease is known as staging. Each type of leukemia has a different staging system, but all indicate the extent to which the disease has progressed. As an example, the Rai staging system for CLL has five stages. The 0 stage is characterized by high numbers of lymphocytes. Stage 1 includes large numbers of lymphocytes and enlarged lymph nodes. In stage 2, an enlarged liver or spleen is added to the stage 1 factors. Stage 3 adds anemia, and stage 4 includes a low platelet count. The higher the stage number, the more advanced a case of CLL is considered to be.

For CML, there are no standardized numbered stages; doctors generally refer only to whether the leukemia is in the chronic, accelerated, or blast-crisis phase. ALL and AML also are not staged according to a formal staging system; rather the subtypes are classified and the treatment formulated according to internationally recognized guidelines called the French-American-British subtype system.

Chapter 2

What Causes Leukemia?

REGARDLESS OF THE particular subtype of leukemia that is diagnosed, "it's pretty infrequent that we know what causes leukemia in an individual,"[8] says Dr. Robert Collins, director of the bone marrow transplant program at the University of Texas Southwestern Medical Center at Dallas. Sometimes, experts say, the disease can be directly traced to specific environmental triggers, but most of the time, the underlying cause is a mystery.

With many types of cancer, scientific research has documented clear and convincing causes; this knowledge enables people to adjust their lifestyle to try to prevent certain cancerous growths, or malignancies. For example, smoking cigarettes has been proven to cause lung cancer, and exposure to the sun is known to produce skin cancers, so many people take steps to protect themselves from these proven risks. But with leukemia, no such obvious measures are available. Right now, according to the American Cancer Society, "there is no known way to prevent most cases of leukemia. Unlike some other types of cancer, most leukemia is not linked to lifestyle risk factors."[9]

Despite the uncertainty over events that might trigger the majority of leukemia cases, scientists have found strong evidence that radiation and some chemicals do play a major role in causing some instances of the disease. Avoiding these risks is obviously a prudent practice, albeit not a guarantee against ever getting leukemia.

Radiation Risks

The first indication that certain types of radiation might be linked to leukemia came in the early 1900s, soon after the discovery of X rays and the first uses of radiation to treat other forms of cancer. Many doctors who administered radiation began getting leukemia. A medical specialist writing for the American Cancer Society takes up the story:

> Many early radiologists used the skin on their arms to test the strength of radiation from their radiotherapy machines, looking for a dose that would produce a pink reaction (erythema) that looked like a sunburn. They called this the "erythema dose", and this was considered an estimate of the proper daily fraction of radiation. In retrospect, it is no surprise that many developed leukemia.[10]

Since these early findings, doctors have proven that people exposed to radiation on the job, during medical treatments for cancer or other disorders, and as a result of exposure to fallout from atomic bombs, have a significantly higher risk of getting leukemia. Many survivors of the World War II atomic bombings in Japan, for example, developed ALL, CLL, or AML two to ten years after the blasts, and the probability of getting leukemia increased with longer and closer exposure to the places the bombs struck. Evidence shows that people located one and one-half miles from the center of a blast had three times the normal incidence of leukemia, while those survivors who were one-quarter mile away were twenty times likelier to get the disease.

Electromagnetic Fields and Leukemia

Although certain types of radiation have been proven to cause leukemia, data on a related suspected cause known as electromagnetic fields, or EMFs, is still being debated and analyzed. EMFs are energy zones that come from high-voltage electric power lines, and, to a lesser degree, from home appliances and faulty electric wiring. They have been suspected of causing leukemia since a 1979 study by doctors Nancy Wertheimer and Ed Leeper of the University of Colorado indicated that many child-

Atomic bombings such as this one, over Nagasaki, Japan, caused many cases of leukemia in areas surrounding the blast.

hood leukemia victims in Denver lived near electric power lines. The presence of a surprisingly high number of cases of a disease in a single area is called clustering.

Since 1979, some studies have supported the contention that EMFs cause leukemia, while others have found no connection. The National Institutes of Health (NIH) recommends that people avoid excessive exposure despite the "lack of consistent positive findings in animal or [other] studies." In its report, the NIH also points out that

> because virtually everyone in the United States uses electricity and therefore is routinely exposed to EMF, efforts to encourage reductions in exposure should continue. For example, industry should continue efforts to alter large transmission lines to reduce their fields and localities should enforce electrical codes to avoid wiring errors that can produce higher fields.[11]

Recent research suggesting that EMFs activate certain cancer-related chemicals in cells has given a boost to the argument that these energy fields may indeed be responsible for some cases of leukemia, but experts continue to affirm that so far no one has actually proven that EMFs cause this disease or any other.

The Chemical Connection

As with data on EMFs, evidence linking some environmental chemicals to leukemia is often inconclusive. Several studies have found that farmers and other agricultural workers exposed to pesticides, herbicides, and fertilizers have a 10 to 40 percent higher incidence of leukemia than other people. But even though leukemia does appear more often in people who have been exposed to these chemicals, experts have not yet established that the chemicals actually cause the disease. A similar situation exists with styrene and butadiene, chemicals used in occupations as diverse as hairstyling, car repair, and rubber making: A link is suspected but not proven.

The chemical called benzene, however, has been conclusively demonstrated to cause leukemia, particularly AML, and its use is strictly regulated by the U.S. Environmental Protection Agency (EPA). Benzene is found in automobile exhaust fumes, petroleum products, industrial solvents, rubber and nylon manufacturing, printing supplies, paint, film developing agents, some glues, and cigarette smoke. It is known to be dangerous when breathed, consumed in drinking water, or absorbed through the skin. People who receive regular exposure on the job get leukemia over twenty times more frequently than most people do, and the EPA says that, despite regulations allowing only minute amounts in air and water samples, virtually all Americans are exposed to some benzene through auto exhaust fumes and first- or second-hand cigarette smoke. In many parts of the world, regulation of benzene is much less stringent, and everyday exposure is even greater.

Although many experts do not consider cigarette smoking to be a direct cause of leukemia, new data on benzene and other cancer-causing chemicals added to cigarettes has prompted the

According to the American Cancer Society, one-fifth of AML cases are caused by smoking.

American Cancer Society to state recently that "about one-fifth of cases of AML are caused by smoking."[12] Avoiding cigarettes is already proven to reduce the risk of lung cancer, heart disease, and other medical problems, so adding leukemia to the list of smoking-related illnesses is, according to the American Cancer Society, yet another reason to stop or never start smoking and to reduce exposure to secondhand smoke.

Leukemia Clusters

Besides its known dangers in cigarettes, gasoline fumes, and various industrial compounds, benzene, along with another toxic chemical called triethylchlorine, has been implicated in several well-publicized leukemia clusters around toxic-waste dump sites. These clusters associated with toxic chemicals are similar to leukemia clusters studied in the early research on EMFs; the difference is that EMFs have not been proven to cause the disease in groups of people exposed to them, while scientific evidence shows that some of the toxic wastes were undoubtedly responsible for causing leukemia.

One of the best-known toxic waste clusters occurred in the 1960s at River Valley High School in Marion, Ohio. The school was built on a former military ammunition and supply dump, and when an unusually high number of River Valley High graduates were diagnosed with leukemia, authorities began to investigate. In 1961, just before the high school was built, the military had burned paint thinner, oil, asbestos, radioactive uranium and radium, trichloroethylene (a solvent used to remove grease), and benzene at the site, and later testing showed that these toxic materials were abundant in the soil and drinking water at the school. After many years of legal battles, former students and their families finally succeeded in having the high school closed down, based on evidence that benzene and trichloroethylene in particular were proven to cause leukemia.

Another abnormally high number of cases of disease in East Woburn, Massachusetts, provided even more evidence linking benzene and trichloroethylene to leukemia in a cluster traced to a food packaging plant, a leather tannery, and an industrial dry cleaning business. A wide variety of chemicals from these businesses were disposed of improperly, contaminating the air, soil, and groundwater and resulting in over four times the expected number of leukemia cases among people who lived nearby. Experts later proved that benzene and trichloroethylene were primarily to blame. In 1979, Boston reporter Dan Kennedy, who had completed over two hundred articles on the East Woburn crisis, identified Anne Anderson, a Woburn mother whose son Jimmy had died of leukemia, as "a national symbol of the fight against corporate carelessness."[13] The story became the basis for the book and movie *A Civil Action,* and since that time the public and government authorities have become more aware of the relationship between these toxic chemicals and leukemia.

Leukemia and the Immune System

Experts now understand that large quantities of toxic substances in areas like East Woburn and Marion cause leukemia by pro-

The film A Civil Action, *starring John Travolta, is based on the toxic waste cluster in East Woburn, Massachusetts. Kathleen Quinlan (right) plays Anne Anderson, an East Woburn mother whose son Jimmy died of leukemia.*

gressively weakening people's immune systems and by wreaking havoc with the DNA in bone marrow cells. The role of a weakened immune system in triggering leukemia is confirmed by recent evidence showing an increased incidence of the disease in people whose immune systems have been weakened by a variety of sources, including, but not limited to, toxic chemicals.

For example, people who must take immunosuppressive drugs to prevent rejection of transplanted organs have a high risk of developing leukemia. So do people whose immune systems are weakened by certain drugs given for other forms of cancer or for autoimmune diseases like arthritis. These drugs, known as alkylating agents, whose effects include the destruction of bone marrow cells important in the immune defense system, have been found to typically cause leukemia within a few years of administration.

Other evidence linking leukemia to a weakened immune system comes from data on viruses that can trigger the disease.

In many animals, certain viruses have been proven to be directly responsible for causing leukemia—for example, the highly contagious feline leukemia virus is known to give cats the disease, and a preventive vaccine is available. In humans, however, no single virus linked to leukemia has been identified, but there are two viruses that scientists have concluded do play a role in some cases of the illness.

Researchers have determined that human T-cell lymphotropic virus type 1 (HTLV-1), the same virus found in the ancient fifteen-hundred-year-old Chilean mummy discovered in the Atamaca Desert, causes ATL, a subtype of CLL. This virus is closely related to HTLV-3, known to be responsible for acquired immune deficiency syndrome (AIDS), but doctors do not believe that HTLV-1 is spread in the same manner as the AIDS virus. No one has found out how HTLV-1 is passed from person to person, but evidence suggests that when people are exposed to it early in life, the virus lies dormant for many years before coming to life to trigger ATL. Not everyone who has the HTLV-1 virus ends up getting leukemia, though, and researchers are presently seeking to determine what protects the healthy carriers.

The second virus linked to human leukemia is the Epstein-Barr virus, which can cause mononucleosis, chronic fatigue syndrome, and other illnesses. As with HTLV-1, not everyone who gets the Epstein-Barr virus develops leukemia, but enough people do for doctors to consider it a known risk factor and likely cause of the disease. It seems that having a disease caused by the Epstein-Barr virus in childhood often means that a person will develop B-cell lymphocytic leukemia later in life. Recent research indicates that the virus not only weakens the immune system, but also inserts itself into the cellular DNA and rearranges the genes and chromosomes.

How Are DNA and Leukemia Related?

Altering a cell's DNA appears to be a common mechanism of action not only for viruses linked to leukemia, but also for other known causes such as radiation and toxic chemicals. While doctors have suspected for some time that changes in the cells themselves are ultimately responsible for inducing leukemia regardless of the underlying cause, only during the past two decades have technological advances enabled experts to gain a better understanding of the exact changes involved.

When Rudolf Virchow first formally identified leukemia in 1845, he was one of the first doctors in the world to relate cells viewed under a microscope to disease processes. Previously, people believed diseases like cancer came exclusively from outside sources such as evil spirits or poisons, which today would be called environmental toxins, rather than from something going wrong with the cells inside a person's body.

Since Virchow's time, experts have discovered a great deal about how normal cells change into cancerous ones, and they have determined that a disruption in the biological process of cell growth and death is the critical factor regardless of whether the underlying trigger is radiation, viruses, toxic chemicals, or of unknown origin.

Since Rudolf Virchow identified leukemia in 1845, scientists such as the one pictured have been using microscopes to learn more about the disease.

A DNA molecule contains genetic material that regulates a cell's growth. Leukemia is the result of an injury to the DNA that causes the cell to multiply continuously.

Normally, the genes regulate a cell's orderly growth, division, and death by ordering certain natural chemicals to be released. These instructions are encoded by the particular sequence of genes on each chromosome. Each human cell normally has forty-six chromosomes housing numerous genes that are each part of a DNA molecule.

When alterations in the DNA base chemicals produce mutations, the genetic instructions can be altered so that a cell will no longer grow, divide, and die in an orderly fashion. These mutations can either be passed on to a baby through the parents' egg and sperm cells or can result from damage to the cell sometime during a living creature's lifetime. According to the Leukemia and Lymphoma Society, in the case of leukemia, "the disease results from an acquired (not inherited) genetic injury to the DNA of a single cell, which becomes abnormally malignant and multiplies continuously."[14]

Whether this acquired injury is provoked by radiation, a virus, toxic chemicals, or unknown sources, it either activates a cancer gene known as an oncogene, or, in some instances, it shuts off a gene that stops cell division. In both cases, the mutation results in a cancer cell that begins reproducing itself, overriding all the body's mechanisms for controlled cell division.

How Do Mutations Alter Chromosomes?

One way in which cancer-causing mutations affect cell division is by producing translocations, which are abnormal breaks in a cell's DNA. In a translocation, DNA from one chromosome becomes detached and then fastens onto a different chromosome. These abnormalities can be assessed by examining bone marrow cells in a laboratory using sophisticated DNA-separating techniques and viewing the damaged or translocated chromosomes under a powerful electron microscope.

There are several confirmed chromosome mutations linked to different types of leukemia; one of the most common is the Philadelphia chromosome abnormality found in 90 percent of CML patients and in some people with other kinds of leukemia. Named the Philadelphia chromosome after its discovery in a laboratory at the University of Pennsylvania School of Medicine in Philadelphia, this mutation consistently appears when a piece of chromosome 22 breaks off and attaches to the bottom of chromosome 9. When cells damaged by this mutation are viewed with an electron microscope, chromosome 22 appears abnormally short and chromosome 9 abnormally long.

In producing a Philadelphia chromosome, the translocation disrupts two genes: one called the Abelson, or ABL, gene on chromosome 9 and the other known as the breakpoint cluster region (BCR) gene on chromosome 22. The mutant gene that results is called BCR-ABL. BCR-ABL causes the affected cell to release tyrosine kinase, an abnormal protein that converts a stem cell that should have matured as a white blood cell into a wildly dividing leukemia cell instead.

What Else Can Contribute to Mutations?

While mutated genes such as BCR-ABL are not inherited directly, as are features like hair color and eye color, there is some evidence that different people's genes may be more susceptible to mutation damage because of inherited factors.

Recent research at the University of California at San Francisco (UCSF), for example, confirms that adequate amounts of folic acid, a B vitamin, are critical in maintaining healthy cells. Previous studies have shown that people who do not consume enough folic acid tend to be especially vulnerable to DNA damage, and the university's website discusses new evidence indicating "that children are protected against different types of leukemia depending on which form of an [inherited] enzyme they have for metabolizing folic acid."[15] The UCSF researchers found that individuals who inherit genes that signal cells to make low levels of an enzyme that destroys folic acid seem to be protected against two subtypes of ALL that result from DNA injuries; they believe the low levels of this enzyme insure that more folic acid stays in cells to guard against this genetic damage.

Other research indicates that people who have naturally high levels of an enzyme called NADPH quinone oxidoreductase are less likely to develop leukemia after exposure to benzene. This enzyme is regulated by a gene that is critical in detoxifying quinones, the chemicals that result from the breakdown of benzene in the body. Experts think that inherited differences in cellular NADPH quinone oxidoreductase may explain why some people get leukemia after minimal exposure to benzene while others will not develop the disease even after prolonged contact with the chemical.

Family Ties

Additional evidence that inherited factors may either protect or make an individual more vulnerable to the genetic changes that underlie leukemia derives from studies on the incidence of various types of leukemia in certain families. CLL, in particular, often strikes multiple members of the same family, whether or not all of the individuals live in the same home or even in a similar environment. Researchers believe that an inherited chromosome weakness may make these families more susceptible to this type of leukemia.

Studies on ALL in identical twins also find a probable hereditary component in some instances. Data shows that when one twin gets ALL before age one, the probability of the other twin also getting the disease is nearly 100 percent. While prenatal damage to the twins' DNA may explain why a baby whose twin develops leukemia seldom escapes the same fate, experts believe that an inherited tendency to acquire this sort of DNA damage is actually behind the phenomenon.

Finally, evidence indicating that inherited factors are at least partially responsible for vulnerability to leukemia comes from studies on genetic diseases known to place individuals at an increased risk for childhood AML. Down syndrome and Fanconi anemia are just two examples of genetic disorders associated with a high risk of this type of leukemia; in fact children under age three with Down syndrome are fourteen times more likely than other children to develop AML. Doctors think that somehow the genetic defects involved in Down syndrome and other

Children with Down syndrome are at greater risk of developing leukemia than other children.

disorders impair the ability of a child's DNA to repair itself and thus to withstand any acquired DNA damage.

The Result of Genetic Understanding

Researchers agree that there is much work to do before all the genetic, cellular, and environmental causes of leukemia are completely understood, but modern knowledge about the DNA damage behind the disease has grown tremendously as new technology develops for viewing and analyzing the tiny genes and chromosomes that direct each cell's activities. In turn, this greater understanding of the microscopic causes for leukemia has led to a virtual revolution in effective treatments which have taken some forms of leukemia from being inevitably fatal to being curable in many cases.

Chapter 3

Leukemia Treatment

A REVOLUTION IN LEUKEMIA treatment began in the early 1940s when scientists started to make rapid progress in developing methods of disrupting cancer-cell growth. Prior to this time, treatment was haphazard, often involving the use of poisons, drugs that had worked on other diseases, and bizarre diets that had no effect on leukemia. Because these therapies were ineffective, the expected survival time for people with acute leukemia was under three months.

Step by step, though, investigators began to piece together new discoveries about the sequence of biochemical processes that enable cancer cells to grow and reproduce. This series of events is known as cellular metabolism, and researchers found that disrupting any step in the sequence can disable or kill cells.

Chemicals or drugs that disrupt a cell's metabolism are called antimetabolites. One of the first scientists to try to synthesize antimetabolites was George Hitchings of Burroughs Wellcome Laboratories in Tuckahoe, New York. Hitchings noted in 1942 that cells require DNA to divide. He reasoned that rapidly dividing cancer cells must have a greater need for DNA than normal cells, and thus an antimetabolite drug should be useful in slowing an invasion of cancer cells.

Rubber Doughnuts and Leukemia Cells

Hitchings and Gertrude Elion, a chemist in his laboratory, began working on putting together an artificial substance that was similar to the nucleic acid bases, the building blocks of DNA, but

41

different enough that it would block the formation of DNA molecules. "We used to call it a rubber doughnut. It looked like the real thing, but it wouldn't work [to make DNA],"[16] Elion explained.

The scientists started testing these antimetabolites, which they called DNA blockers, on leukemia cells, and by 1948 had made enough progress to send an experimental drug to Dr. Joseph Burchenal at the Memorial Sloan-Kettering Hospital in New York for testing on leukemia patients. Two adult patients did achieve a remission, or temporary absence of symptoms, but the drug was far too toxic for most people: that is, it made many of the patients sicker.

Elion then modified the antimetabolite into a less toxic form called 6-mercaptopurine, or 6-MP, and the first truly effective

Dr. Joseph Burchenal (second from right) holds an award for the advancement of cancer research. He administered Hitchings and Elion's drug 6-MP to leukemia patients at Memorial Sloan-Kettering Hospital, producing remissions in many cases.

weapon against acute lymphocytic leukemia was created. Although 6-MP also had some toxic effects on normal cells, it produced remissions in many of Dr. Burchenal's patients.

The encouraging results obtained at Memorial Sloan-Kettering sent shock waves through the medical community, as described on the National Academy of Science website:

> In the few days after news of the clinical success with 6-MP broke, Hitchings received over 600 phone calls. The excitement about 6-MP was so great that the U.S. Food and Drug Administration approved its use late in 1953—only 10 months after clinical trials began, and 7 months before all the data supporting its effectiveness were made public.[17]

Elion and Hitchings received the Nobel Prize in medicine in 1988 for their breakthrough.

Other New Approaches

Meanwhile, another group of researchers led by Sidney Farber at the Children's Hospital in Boston was investigating the effects of folic acid on cancer. These scientists developed a folic-acid blocking antimetabolite called aminopterin, which induced temporary remissions in several children with leukemia. Other researchers then worked on developing a similar drug that would give longer-lasting remissions and came up with methotrexate, a potent new weapon against leukemia cells.

Doctors began treating childhood leukemia with both 6-MP and methotrexate, and the average survival time went from two to three months to one year after diagnosis. Even though the two drugs put many patients into remission, the leukemia almost always returned, and this treatment approach, called chemotherapy, was not effective the second time around. Since the drugs acted on normal cells as well as on leukemia cells, there were also traumatic additional effects such as nausea, vomiting, hair loss, and bleeding.

Along with searching for better drugs, physicians began to test various dosages, frequency of administration, and exact combinations to try to extend patients' remissions and minimize the drastic adverse effects of chemotherapy. Beginning in 1955, doctors Emil Frei III and Emil J. Freireich at the National Cancer Institute (NCI) headed the new nationwide drug trials designed to scientifically improve leukemia treatment. Their efforts began with implementing new scientific research techniques that accurately assessed whether or not particular drug combinations were truly effective.

Then, Frei and Freireich edged closer to a permanent cure for ALL when they found that giving patients blood platelet transfusions helped prevent serious bleeding, so patients could endure a longer course of chemotherapy. This practice soon became a standard part of leukemia therapy.

In addition, the NCI team sought to extend patients' remissions by using new data concerning the dangers of not eradicating every single leukemia cell. When researchers at the Southern Research Institute discovered that leaving even one cancer cell alive could cause a later recurrence of the disease, Frei and Freireich redefined a remission as meaning that a patient's bone marrow was free of leukemia cells. Previously, medical experts had considered a person to be in remission when no noticeable symptoms were present. The new criteria led doctors to routinely continue giving chemotherapy past the time when all symptoms had disappeared.

As if to confirm the validity of the continuation of chemotheraphy in apparently symptom-free patients, several researchers soon discovered that even when a patient's blood and bone marrow contained no leukemia cells, the cancer could still be hiding in the central nervous system, which consists of the brain and spinal cord. Since drugs that are swallowed or injected do not reach the central nervous system because of a mechanism known as the blood-brain barrier, the National Academy of Science explains that "doctors therefore began to inject drugs directly into the spinal canal and to target radiation specifically to the head."[18]

Modern Treatment

The combination of spinal injections, radiation, chemotherapy drugs, and blood transfusions soon turned ALL from being rapidly fatal to being completely curable in many patients. These treatments have not worked nearly as well for the other types of leukemia, but since these early advances in the 1950's, the development of other new drugs and other new treatments has rendered AML, CML, and CLL curable in some cases.

The number of cases cured depends on the type and subtype of the disease and on the age of the patient. For children with ALL, for example, the overall five-year survival rate is now about 81 percent. For children with AML it is 43 percent. This is considerably higher than the overall survival rates when adults are included in the statistics; for ALL the overall five-year survival rate is 58 percent; for AML it is 14 percent; for CLL it is 71 percent; and for CML it is 32 percent. Once a patient survives symptom-free with normal blood and bone marrow for five years, doctors consider them cured.

Children with leukemia have a higher five-year survival rate than adults with the disease.

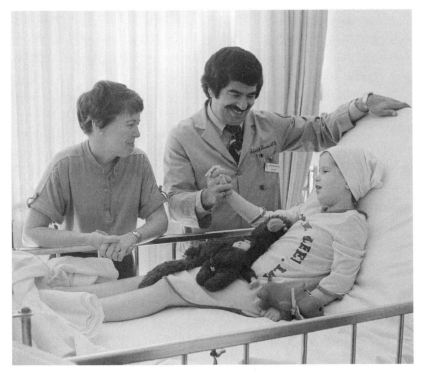

In general, physicians say that the chances of a complete cure are best for the youngest patients whose white blood cell counts are low at the time of diagnosis. Cures are also more likely when the affected white blood cells are B lymphocytes. In addition, acute leukemias are considered to be permanently curable with chemotherapy, while chronic leukemias generally require even more radical measures such as bone marrow transplants for a lasting cure.

Recently, the development of several new blood tests has given doctors further ways of predicting the likelihood of a cure in a particular case. These include chromosome mutation tests and tests which identify antigens and antibodies on the leukemia cells. Such tests can assess the degree of aggressiveness of the leukemia and indicate how well a patient is likely to respond to different drugs.

Beginning Treatment

Armed with multiple test results, along with knowledge about the subtype, stage of the disease, and age and overall health of the patient, a physician will then recommend a course of treatment, also known as a treatment protocol. For acute leukemias, the grueling treatment will begin immediately, while with some chronic cases it can be delayed to see if symptoms and blood counts worsen. Some patients with chronic leukemia do not experience dangerous symptoms or critically abnormal blood counts for several years; in such cases physicians often recommend a "wait-and-see" approach so the patient will not have to endure painful and debilitating therapy until it is absolutely necessary. Either way, the patient, doctor, and family must weigh the chances of recovery, risks, pain and suffering, and temporary or permanent disabilities caused by chemotherapy drugs before deciding on exactly which treatment plan to follow.

According to NCI, "Treatment for leukemia is complex. It varies with the type of leukemia and is not the same for all patients. The doctor plans the treatment to fit each patient's needs."[19] Some patients, for instance, are stronger than others and can receive treatment in the doctor's office or as a hospital outpatient, while others must be hospitalized for weeks or months at a time. The length and frequency of therapy for each person varies too, depending on the drugs and other methods used and on the patient's response. Some treatment plans call for daily injections or pills, while others can be given weekly or monthly for several months.

Patients whose illness is likely to respond to treatment, such as children from one to nine years old with low white cell counts, may be given less toxic drugs, whereas those patients who have a mutation like the Philadelphia chromosome are treated more aggressively with stronger drugs.

Phases of Treatment

Whichever course of treatment a physician prescribes, leukemia therapy has three phases known as induction, consolidation, and

Because the treatment for leukemia varies with each individual, patient and doctor must weigh factors such as the chances of recovery and the risks involved before deciding on a specific treatment plan.

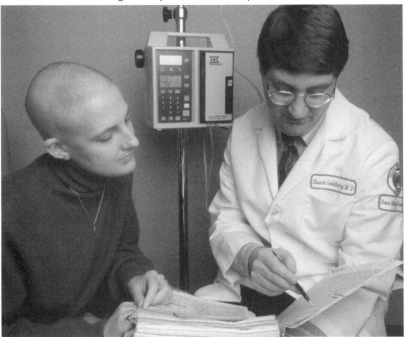

maintenance. In the induction phase, the goal is to kill as many cancer cells as possible and to put the patient into a remission. With different forms of leukemia, different percentages of leukemia cells remaining in the bone marrow are considered acceptable for a remission; for example, with chronic leukemias it is not unusual for the patient to have 10 to 15 percent leukemia cells among the normal white blood cells, whereas with the acute forms of the disease it is unacceptable to have any cancer cells remaining after treatment.

In the consolidation phase, the aim is to destroy any stray cancer cells and prevent a relapse, or recurrence. The maintenance phase involves keeping the patient free of leukemia through ongoing checkups and continuing medication if necessary.

If a relapse occurs following a remission, the physician must then determine whether a new treatment plan is likely to help the patient. Experts define a relapse as a return of the leukemia after thirty or more days of remission, as indicated by the appearance of cancer cells in the blood or marrow and/or the return of any symptoms. Sometimes a relapse happens because all the leukemia cells were not killed the first time around; other times accidental exposure to toxic chemicals or radiation triggers it, and in still other cases the cause is unknown.

Doctors also refer to refractory leukemia, the name given to stubborn cases in which a remission is never achieved. After each failed treatment, another type of drug or therapy is usually tried.

Modern Drug Treatment

The most common first-round method of getting a leukemia patient into remission is the use of a combination of chemotherapy drugs. Like the original 6-MP and methotrexate anticancer drugs, all of these chemotherapy medications work by interfering with a cancer cell's ability to grow and divide, though there are now several different classes of drugs whose exact mechanism of action varies slightly.

Besides the early antimetabolites 6-MP and methotrexate, doctors now use newer drugs like L-asparaginase, cytosine arabinoside, fludarabine, and cladribine to achieve the same purpose. A closely related class of drugs known as DNA-damaging agents work by attaching to the cell's DNA so it can no longer divide; this ideally stops a cancer cell from proliferating and therefore renders it harmless. An example of such a DNA-damaging agent is carboplatinum. Chlorambucil and cyclophosphamide, members of a subclass of DNA-damaging drugs referred to as alkylating agents, are designed to destroy bone marrow cells by inflicting so much DNA damage that these cells die outright.

Antitumor antibiotics are another type of chemotherapy drug that either disables or kills a cell by latching onto the DNA. These include daunorubicin, doxorubicin, and bleomycin. The kind of antibiotic used to kill bacterial infections differs in important respects from the antibiotics designed to kill cancer cells.

Another method of attacking cancer cells is to use DNA-repair-enzyme inhibitors. These drugs damage the proteins needed to repair DNA and thus make the cells more susceptible to destruction from other chemotherapy agents. DNA-repair-enzyme inhibitors such as etoposide and topotecan are often given in combination with several other drugs.

Tubulin-binding agents such as vincristine and vinblastine represent still another class of chemotherapy drugs. These compounds are designed to stop the structures that pull together newly formed chromosomes from acting, thereby halting cell division. Tubulin-binding agents are frequently used in combination with other anticancer medications.

In addition to the other types of drugs used to fight leukemia, hormones like prednisone and other steroids are also sometimes employed as chemotherapy drugs since high doses will kill cancer cells.

How Chemotherapy Is Administered

Different chemotherapy drugs are given in different ways, though most are delivered through an intravenous (IV) tube in an arm vein or through an indwelling catheter, also referred to as a central catheter. A central or indwelling catheter is a flexible tube surgically implanted into a large vein near the heart. It is used in cases where a long course of therapy is expected, since the device avoids having to keep putting IV needles into the arm at each treatment session. This makes chemotherapy safer because the drugs are distributed faster and more evenly throughout the body. A central catheter also eliminates damage to the arm veins from chemotherapy agents that tend to destroy delicate tissue, and in addition makes it easier to administer the frequent blood transfusions needed by leukemia patients.

Some chemotherapy drugs can be given orally in the form of a pill or liquid, injected into a muscle, or given through a tiny computerized pump that is implanted under the skin and stores the medicine until a timer triggers it to release a certain amount. Patients who are on these medications may be able to take the drugs at home or as a hospital outpatient.

A young girl receives a chemotherapy injection.

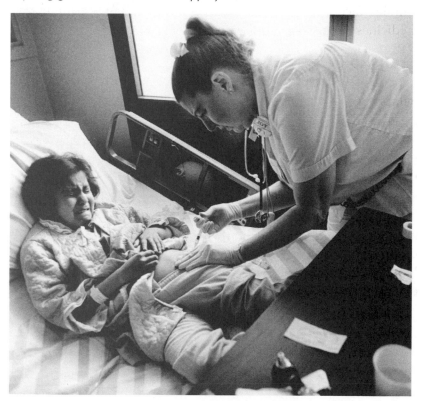

Sometimes chemotherapy drugs such as methotrexate must be injected directly into the spinal fluid to eradicate cancer cells in the nervous system. This process, called an intrathecal injection, is done only in hospitals. Rather than risking repeated spinal injections in critically ill patients, physicians often implant a holding container called an Omaya reservoir underneath the scalp.

The Financial Toll

Whichever method of administration is used, chemotherapy drugs are extremely expensive, particularly the newer drugs, which may cost several hundred dollars per dose. Along with the other costs involved in diagnosis and treatment, these fees can impose an extreme burden on families even when they have medical insurance, since some insurance plans do not cover the more expensive options. Sometimes drug companies and research facilities offer assistance programs, but in many cases, families face financial ruin from absorbing the costs of these medicines and associated fees like hospital stays.

Drugs to Reduce Unwanted Effects of Chemotherapy

Along with the burden of expense, another hardship chemotherapy patients face is that the drugs designed to attack cancer cells also produce extensive effects on cells that had been functioning properly. Depending on the particular drug and dosage, these so-called side effects can include an impaired immune system, damage to the heart, liver, kidneys, and other organs, a slowing of children's growth, seizures, fever, paralysis, numbness, bone and limb pain, infertility, hair loss, nausea, vomiting, diarrhea, mouth sores, low blood counts, and sometimes death. Recalls AML survivor Annette of her near-fatal chemotherapy experience:

> I was in the hospital for about five weeks. I experienced about every side effect of treatment. I was extremely nauseated. I had constant diarrhea, I called it toxic sludge, and I vomited. I experienced nadir, where all my blood counts bottomed out for one and a half to two weeks, and I ran high fevers at 105 degrees.

The chills were so vicious I would almost go into convulsion. I lost my hair and it was so frightening for me to look in the mirror. I think half the battle for me was just believing I would make it through, even the darkest hour.[20]

To control some of these undesirable effects of chemotherapy, doctors often administer other medications along with the anticancer drugs. Antinausea drugs like Zofran are commonly used to cut down on debilitating nausea and vomiting. Steroids like prednisone are often used to lengthen the survival time of red blood cells and platelets to increase blood counts. Rescue drugs such as leucovorin, a form of the B vitamin folinic acid that allows normal cells to rebuild their DNA; allopurinol, a drug that helps the kidneys flush out chemotherapy agents; and mesna, which protects the bladder from bleeding and infection brought on by chemotherapy, are among the medicines given to lessen the unpleasant effects of potentially lifesaving drugs.

Other Leukemia Treatments

Along with the standard chemotherapy and medications to control unwanted effects, there are several other treatment procedures that doctors administer to many leukemia patients. One is leukapheresis, a technique where the patient's blood is circulated through a machine that filters out cancerous white blood cells and recirculates the rest of the blood back into the bloodstream. This technique is used to reduce dangerously high white cell counts while the patient is beginning chemotherapy.

A badly inflamed spleen or very swollen lymph nodes will be surgically removed, but this is merely to alleviate the leukemia patient's pain and does not take the place of chemotherapy in an attempt to eradicate the cancer.

Radiation therapy is used as needed to kill leukemia cells that have spread to the brain and spinal cord. A specialist known as a radiation oncologist determines the appropriate radiation dosage and frequency. To reduce serious side effects as much as possible, the patient receives numerous radiation sessions over several weeks by means of a a linear accelerator, which narrowly focuses a high voltage ray at a particular spot.

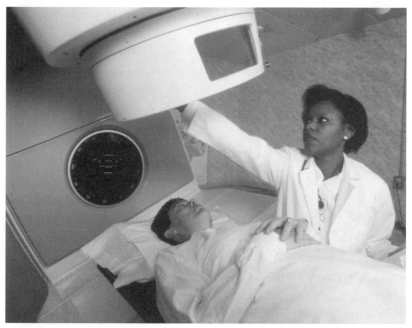

Radiation therapy is a form of treatment that kills malignant cells that have spread to the brain and spinal cord.

The radiation prevents cancer cells from reproducing by injuring or destroying their DNA. Like chemotherapy, radiation can also affect normal cells and result in similar unwanted effects, along with the problems of eye soreness and cataracts, skin burning, rashes, memory impairment, and hormone abnormalities. In addition, radiation treatments are proven to increase the risk of other types of cancer, so they must be done sparingly and carefully.

Bone Marrow Transplants

When chemotherapy and radiation treatments fail, many patients today go on to have bone marrow or stem-cell transplants. Some patients elect to undergo these procedures even when other treatments work well, in the hopes that they will not get a relapse. In cases of CLL and CML, some patients have a transplant early on in hopes of preventing the chronic phase of their leukemia from becoming acute.

Although transplants cure many patients and are classified as standard leukemia treatments, some medical insurers consider them experimental and refuse to cover the $100,000 to $200,000 costs. Many families then either take legal action against the insurer or try to get a free transplant through NIH, the National Cancer Center, or other institutions that sponsor such programs.

Bone marrow transplants have been in existence for about thirty years, and modern improvements have made them safer and more likely to be successful than they used to be. Still, they remain extremely risky. Even today, only about 45 percent of children and 10 to 30 percent of adults who receive them survive, but for many, the risky procedure offers the only ray of hope. "I knew I might die during the transplant, but I tried not to think about that and focused on how it would help me,"[21] says bone marrow-transplant survivor Baruch Margalit, who had the procedure to avoid getting a relapse of AML.

Bone marrow transplants can be done only at highly specialized hospital facilities called transplant centers. The transplanted marrow may come from the patient, or it may be donated. The material for autologous transplants, those that use the patient's own marrow, is extracted with a needle while the patient is in remission after chemotherapy. This delicate procedure, which is called harvesting, is similar to a bone marrow aspiration. If there are any leukemia cells in the harvested marrow, the doctors may order the hospital laboratory to kill these cells with chemotherapy drugs, a process known as purging the marrow.

Once the marrow is harvested and purged, if necessary, the patient gets high doses of chemotherapy and radiation to obliterate all the remaining marrow. Since the procedure completely destroys the immune system, the patient must be isolated in a germ-free room until the harvested marrow is injected and becomes engrafted into the bone cavities, where it starts to spread and produce blood cells. This can take over a month, during which time all doctors, nurses, and visitors must wear masks, shoe coverings, and gowns. Laments one man who went through a bone marrow transplant for CLL, "I am stuck here,

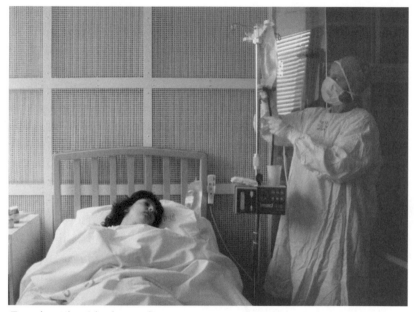

To reduce the risk of spreading germs to a patient whose immune system is suppressed, those who enter the sterile environment of a bone marrow transplant unit must wear protective clothing.

my only constant companion an IV tree holding the bags of one thing or another that flow through the tubes planted in my chest. As my visitors leave, I find myself envying their freedom. They can't know the isolation I am enduring."[22] Even after the period of extreme isolation ends, the patient often must remain hospitalized for additional weeks or months until the new marrow functions properly and the immune system begins working again.

When the patient's own marrow cannot be used, transplant material is donated by another person, usually a brother or sister with the same tissue type or an unrelated donor who is tissue-type matched through the National Marrow Donor Program registry. In these procedures, called allogeneic transplants, matches are made by examining antigens on the white blood cells. Recipients must take drugs that suppress the immune system to prevent their body from rejecting the donated cells, no matter how closely they are matched. Even with immunosuppressive drugs,

some patients' bodies reject the donor marrow with horrific con-
sequences, including blood loss, weight loss, cramps, nausea,
and even death.

Elderly CML and CLL patients often are considered too frail to
withstand a full bone marrow transplant. In such cases, doctors
may perform a new type of allogeneic transplant called a mini-
transplant, where the patient's bone marrow is not totally de-
stroyed. Even this procedure is considered risky; like other
transplants, it can be fatal and requires long periods of isolation
and follow-up care.

Stem-Cell Transplants

A newer type of transplant known as a stem-cell transplant has
been developed over the past decade to provide another option
for patients seeking a leukemia cure. Like transplanted bone
marrow, transplanted blood-forming stem cells are administered
after the patient's own marrow is damaged or obliterated by high
doses of chemotherapy and radiation. The stem cells become engrafted into the recipient's remaining bone marrow and should
enable the person's body to begin producing normal blood cells.
Unlike a bone marrow transplant, though, the cells to be transplanted in a stem-cell transplant come from blood rather than directly from bone marrow.

The technique uses stem cells from the patient's own blood,
from a donor's blood, or from the placental or umbilical-cord
blood of a newborn baby. In most modern cultures, the placenta
and umbilical cord are usually discarded after birth, but since researchers discovered that these tissues can be used as sources of
stem cells, many medical centers now freeze and store the essential components for later use in transplants.

Alternative and Complementary Treatment

When the modern arsenal of transplants, chemotherapy, and
other procedures fail to help a particular patient, or when the
person wishes to avoid the unpleasant effects associated with
these difficult treatments, some individuals are driven to desper-
ation and will try just about anything in an attempt to cure their

leukemia. Such patients sometimes fall prey to charlatans touting miracle cures or try unproven therapies that do nothing to help them. Some individuals try various vitamins or herbs that are advertised as cures, while others go to unlicensed clinics in various places around the world. Leukemia experts strongly caution patients against substituting such unproven methods for medically approved procedures.

However, doctors have realized that there are some legitimate complementary practices that may be beneficial when administered by licensed practitioners and used in conjunction with accepted medical protocols. These include acupuncture, biofeedback, yoga, massage therapy, meditation, and psychotherapy.

Acupuncture, an ancient Chinese healing system that balances the body's energy by stimulating appropriate points on the skin

Acupuncture can alleviate side effects of chemotherapy and strengthen the immune system by stimulating points on the skin.

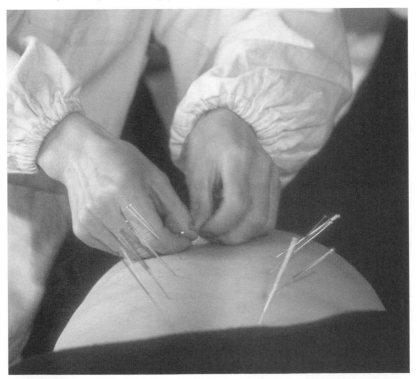

with fine needles, has been shown to help alleviate the unwanted effects of chemotherapy, strengthen the immune system, and relieve the stress and pain associated with the disease. Massage therapy, yoga, meditation, and biofeedback, a technique where people learn to control certain aspects of their biological functioning such as pain and heart rate, are found to help in a similar manner.

Counseling with a psychotherapist or social worker to help patients deal with the many stresses and lifestyle issues associated with leukemia are also proven to be extremely helpful to many patients and their families and are an integral part of leukemia treatment at many hospitals and cancer treatment centers.

Chapter 4

Living with Leukemia

WHATEVER THE TYPE of leukemia and the treatment process may be, leukemia patients and their families face drastic changes in lifestyle, goals, priorities, and emotional health from the moment of diagnosis onward. Suddenly work, play, and relationships become centered around medical procedures and hospitals as the patient and family set off to defeat a terrifying enemy. For all involved, living with leukemia is a major challenge that can take various paths depending on the individuals, the prognosis, and the treatment results. Ann, a survivor of childhood ALL, writes:

> After a diagnosis of cancer, your life will never be the same again. You will understand what it really means to be scared, and at the same time you will learn to notice the beauty in the everyday world. It is a battle of extremes. . . . Cancer can be a stumbling block in the road of life, but it also grants you an opportunity that you did not have before. You can decide what is really important to you.[23]

Like Ann, some leukemia survivors choose to focus on spiritual and personal growth opportunities in an effort to overcome the dizzying array of emotions and disruptions that go along with leukemia. Many of these survivors go on to lead productive lives that hold a renewed sense of purpose and vigor. Other leukemia patients and their loved ones never climb out of the chasm of despair which the diagnosis inspires, and this may result in persistent depression and an inability to find meaning or purpose in life.

Common Reactions to a Diagnosis of Leukemia

Experts report that common emotional reactions to the initial diagnosis may include guilt over lifestyle habits or faulty genes that may have triggered the disease, anger at God that may progress to a loss of faith, denial of the disease, or anger at a particular person. Children too young to understand that nothing they or anyone else did is responsible for the disease are especially likely to have trouble with anger. One four-year-old, for example, thought her leukemia was her doctor's fault and lashed out at the doctor. A puzzled ten-year-old boy asked his parents why God was punishing him with leukemia.

Parents of children with the disease have a particularly difficult time making adjustments and coping with the diagnosis as well, say experts, since a life-threatening illness and the possibility of death in a child are among the worst things that can happen to a parent. Social workers Pennie Heath and Frances Greeson explain:

The diagnosis of leukemia in a child can be particularly hard on parents, who must cope with financial and familial worries in addition to concerns about their child.

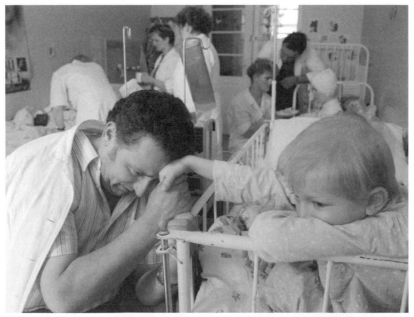

To have a child diagnosed with cancer is to learn to live with chronic sorrow. You grieve for the loss of your previously healthy child, for the loss of your normal daily routine, for the impact of the illness on your family, for the financial losses you will incur, for not being able to return to work or school and for so many other things.[24]

Social Forces in Coping with Diagnosis

Regardless of whether the patient is a child, teen, or adult, leukemia survivors report that the love and support of family and friends were crucial in helping them find the strength to deal with the trauma of diagnosis and to go on living as productive human beings. Baruch, who survived AML and a bone marrow transplant when he was in his late forties, found his outlook on life permanently changed for the better upon witnessing the reaction of people around him to his diagnosis:

> When I was first diagnosed with AML and was so sick in the hospital for a month, I was inundated with incredible amounts of love and care and help from my family, friends, acquaintances, and professional colleagues in the community. It was a major turning point for me. It let me know just how good people can be. This positive experience has sustained me ever since. It's made me feel very much a part of humanity and much more positive in general.[25]

Not everyone, however, is as fortunate as Baruch was in receiving loving support from others. Sometimes family members, friends, schoolmates, or coworkers are unable to respond supportively in the presence of a terrifying disease like leukemia and instead act distant and uncaring or, in some cases, are so hysterical that they harm the patient's ability to cope. Mental health experts explain that often this is because people are so frightened or uncertain that they do not know what to do or how to act, but in any case they end up making the patient feel abandoned, resentful, or isolated.

Marquita, who was diagnosed with ALL at age twelve, considers herself lucky that her true friends stuck by her even when many

A cancer-stricken teenager plays with her family. Family and friends are an important source of support for leukemia patients.

so-called friends suddenly dropped her when she got sick. "I lost a lot of friends during that time; I'm not sure why. Maybe they were afraid they would 'catch' it from me. But not all my friends ran off, and I am grateful for the ones that stood by me,"[26] she says.

Support Services

With all the emotional, social, and practical changes that a diagnosis of leukemia forces on an individual's and family's lifestyle, professionals who work with leukemia patients and survivors alike say there are many ways of making the adaptation a bit easier.

Many cancer treatment centers have special nurses and social workers to help people deal with the many lifestyle questions that arise; there are also independent counselors who specialize in cancer-related therapy, and in some areas there are experts who are affiliated with organizations like Cancer Family Care. In addition, many people find they benefit immensely from joining a support group, where they can exchange information and discuss their feelings with others who are going through or have been through a similar situation. Some support groups are part of national organizations, such as the Leukemia Society of America, and offer online and telephone information as well as local chapters. Other groups are organized by local hospitals or individuals. There are also many informal online chat groups and buddy services that are not part of any official support group but often provide invaluable sources of compassion and coping skills.

Professional counselors and support groups can help patients and families deal with every imaginable issue, from who to tell about a diagnosis of leukemia to what to do when treatment fails. One question that virtually always comes up, for example, is whether or not to tell every family member, friend, or coworker about the diagnosis. While there are no easy answers that apply to everyone, patient advocates and experienced veterans say that usually it is wise to inform close family members and friends, children's teachers, and some coworkers such as the boss, but that it is not necessary to share details except with immediate family. Of course, experts emphasize that the age of family members must be considered before deciding how much to reveal; small children will not understand many details and may easily become very frightened by graphic specifics. Nevertheless, counselors say it is still important that even young children be told something is wrong and assured that, regardless of what happens, they will continue to be loved and cared for.

Navigating the Leukemia Journey

Survivors and experts agree that taking control of challenges like who to inform about the disease is a critical step in turning an overwhelming tragedy into a difficult life situation that can be addressed step by step. Indeed, say social worker Sally Wiard and medical doctor Sachin Jogal, learning to judge which aspects of the leukemia journey can and cannot be controlled is a big part of living with the disease.

It is important to try to begin to differentiate between things that you can and cannot control. This allows you to set goals and to solve problems in a more realistic fashion. . . . Setting realistic limits can help you to cope at any time in life, but it may be especially important in times of stress and change. It is good to try to live one day at a time. Sometimes, during periods of intense stress, the time frame may even need to be one hour at a time.[27]

Gary, a young father who survived AML, initially felt overwhelmed after he was diagnosed, but made a determined effort to control his attitude to make the entire process easier on himself and his family.

I made up my mind that I was going to beat the odds. . . . I developed some thoughts during the first traumatic 48 hours that helped me focus on what had to be done to attempt a sane survival of the disease and treatment. . . . I believe that these concepts helped me survive the treatment with my sanity intact. They also made it easier for care team members to see me as a real person, and it was less stressful for my family.[28]

Other patients use a variety of ways of taking some control over the ordeal; these may involve tried-and-true ways of promoting positive thinking, including meditation, yoga, reading inspiring books, listening to music, writing in a journal, sharing time with a precious pet or with a person whose outlook is consistently positive, praying, and other techniques that may work for different individuals.

Visualization, a technique taught by many psychotherapists who deal with cancer patients, is another common method of helping people gain some sense of control over their leukemia journey. In visualization, patients are trained to imagine that their immune cells are attacking the leukemia cells, and scientific studies have shown this practice can significantly bolster patients' spirits and make lifestyle changes less traumatic. Some experts argue that the practice also helps leukemia treatments work more effectively, but so far it remains unproven whether the visualization process itself or the overall positive mental attitude is responsible for any therapeutic medical results.

A woman plays guitar in a cancer ward. Listening to music is one way leukemia patients cope with the pain and suffering caused by the illness.

After the Diagnosis

In addition to the need to cope with the shock of a diagnosis of leukemia, experts say there are several immediate decisions to make that can ease the entire ordeal for the patient and family. The first step in making the experience as tolerable as possible is to find an oncologist or hematologist who not only has excellent medical qualifications, but also communicates effectively with everyone involved. Some patients and families like to receive detailed explanations about everything related to therapy, while others prefer to rely solely on the doctor's expertise in planning a course of action. Patient advocates state that it is important to let the doctor know about any preferences in this regard, and also to be sure that the physician is willing to assist individuals who wish to obtain detailed knowledge online or in books about the disease.

When choosing a doctor, good communication skills are often just as important to the patient as the physician's medical expertise.

Personality factors are also critical in deciding which doctor to entrust with care and treatment. A tendency to present information and treat patients in a condescending manner is likely to create an unsatisfactory climate for healing. Therefore, patient advocates encourage people to look for a doctor who shows compassion and awareness of emotional needs as well as being a qualified expert on leukemia. Some medical insurance plans will pay for consults with several specialists if a patient does not feel comfortable with the first doctor he or she visits; other times it is more practical to seek a recommendation from a trusted family physician or from a local family that has experienced a similar disease. In cases where there is only one cancer specialist in a small community, it may become necessary for a patient to travel to an out-of-town medical center to find a satisfactory doctor.

Along with hiring a doctor who best meets any medical and emotional needs, the choice of a particular hospital or cancer-care clinic is another critical decision that can play a big role in making life with leukemia easier. For some individuals, traveling outside the local area may be impossible, and it is necessary to accept whatever care is available close by. But for those who have the option of searching for the best possible clinic, there are several important factors to consider. Some facilities are better than others in providing support services and in helping patients and families respond to the many medical emergencies that are a part of living with the disease. Some will even assist with arrangements for at-home care when the patient is recovering at home or takes a turn for the worse and does not want to return to the hospital, and some are well equipped to make referrals to specialized hospitals in other locations when necessary. Adult patients may need help preparing documents such as a living will and a medical power of attorney that specify the patient's wishes as to who will make decisions if he or she becomes totally incapacitated. Finding a care center that offers this type of assistance can make this aspect of living with leukemia progress more smoothly.

Lifestyle Upsets During Treatment

Dealing with the many changes initiated by a diagnosis of leukemia is difficult enough, but patients and their loved ones say that coping with the treatment process is even more grueling socially, emotionally, and physically. Socially, being confined to a hospital and missing school, work, and other activities can take a huge toll on an individual's and family's ties to other people, even when friends and coworkers are supportive. Experts say that children's social development, in particular, often suffers from the necessity of being hospitalized for long periods of time and having to be careful about catching infections even when they are out of the hospital. Many children must have private tutors and tend to feel isolated from their classmates; sometimes they feel left out even after returning to school, when the physical debilitation from the disease may keep them from participating in sports and other activities they previously enjoyed.

For any leukemia patient, beginning and continuing necessary treatment creates lifestyle upsets that extend beyond feeling left out or having to stop doing things that were once taken for granted. Besides making critical decisions about chemotherapy and other treatment options, patients and families must wrestle with practical matters like who will care for children, do housework, cook meals, transport the patient places, and stay with the patient in the hospital if needed. If the patient is a child, this almost always means that one parent must be at the hospital at all times; other family members and friends then must help with caring for any other children in the family. If the patient is an adult who works or cares for a family, making arrangements for time off can be stressful and unsettling. Most employed persons have some sick-leave time, but many lose pay and promotions when they cannot work for long periods.

A child with leukemia is comforted by his mother. Because parents often need time off from work to care for their children, a diagnosis of leukemia can cause financial hardships.

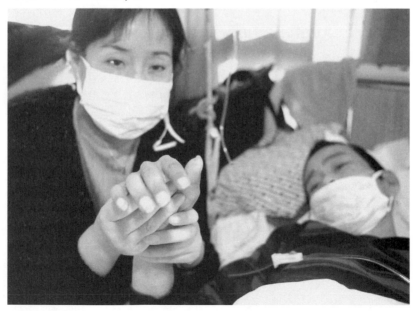

Cancer is designated as a disability under the Americans with Disabilities Act, and anyone harmed professionally or emotionally on the job as a result of the illness can seek legal recourse. But taking legal action can be extremely expensive, time-consuming, and physically impossible for someone facing a traumatic course of treatment and recovery.

For many adults in particular, accepting help with the financial, practical, and emotional challenges during treatment is a very difficult adjustment as well. Mike, for example, was embarrassed when his coworkers and community members organized and hosted a fund-raising barbecue to help pay for his bone marrow transplant. Graciously accepting the outpouring of support was difficult for this independent man who was usually the one to offer assistance to others, but he managed to do so when he realized how much people wanted to help.

Annette, who survived AML after nearly dying from complications of chemotherapy, reveals, "I felt so vulnerable and completely dependent on everyone . . . the most important lesson I had to learn was to accept assistance from others. I had to learn to be humble and take back strength from the kindness of my family."[29]

After Treatment

Even after treatment is completed, a patient's and family's life does not return to the way it was previously. "The leukemia experience doesn't end when treatment ends. It now requires a new kind of normalcy,"[30] says CLL survivor Barbara Lackritz in her book *Adult Leukemia*.

This new normalcy may include frequent medical appointments to monitor the patient's condition and to make sure they do not relapse, along with changes in priorities and in physical and emotional functioning. Many survivors report, for example, that suddenly things like getting a new car or buying the coolest clothes no longer matter. Instead, communicating one's feelings and spending time with family and friends become the central focus in life.

Other individuals have ongoing psychological disorders similar to post-traumatic stress disorder, a condition common in victims of war and other tragic occurrences. Many experience ongoing insomnia, nightmares, and depression from memories of their treatment experience and from fears that the disease will return. Experts say that sometimes families unknowingly encourage this sort of emotional malaise by overprotecting and making an invalid out of a loved one who has survived leukemia; in other cases the family's unrealistic expectations that the patient will bounce right back to normal can lead to such emotional difficulties.

The prospect of a relapse in particular is reported to be a significant source of ongoing stress for both patients and families living with the aftermath of leukemia, and if a relapse actually takes place it can force the anxiety level to a new high. Steve, who experienced a relapse four months after surviving a bone marrow transplant, remembers:

> Compared to this news, what I felt when I first heard that I had been diagnosed with leukemia was just a stroll in the park. Memories of the all-too-frequent and painful spinal taps, hours and hours of receiving blood products, vomiting, pain, loss of my hair, and the loss of my dignity all filled my head. This news put the fear of God in me instantly. It was an overwhelming fear, and it was terrifying. Suddenly my whole life changed for the second time.[31]

Ongoing Problems

In addition to the emotional trauma of post-treatment life, leukemia survivors may also face a variety of ongoing physical problems that force them to further change their lifestyle and priorities. Some of these problems may be present right after treatment ends, while others known as late effects may develop later on as a result of chemotherapy or other procedures. Baruch, for instance, developed diabetes, osteoporosis (a weakening of the bones), cataracts in his eyes, and scleroderma (a disabling autoimmune disease that affects the skin and internal organs) over several years as a result of complications following a bone marrow transplant. He had to retire from his job as a psychotherapist, along with giving up his participation in the sports he previously enjoyed. Many other patients have permanent pain from certain chemotherapy drugs and also must alter their activities accordingly. The drug vincristine, for example, can lead to lifelong pain in the hands and feet from nerve damage. Other drugs may damage nerves in the eyes and ears, resulting in vision and hearing problems, and sometimes effects on the nerves in the brain lead to severe learning, memory, and behavior difficulties and the need for special education for children. Doctors say that very young children who receive several rounds of chemotherapy and radiation are especially vulnerable to these effects.

Immune-system damage from leukemia treatment leaves many people with new allergies, including food allergies that force them to alter their eating habits. The weakening of the immune system can also lead to a chronic inability to fight off colds

Chemotherapy and radiation treatment can cause learning, memory, and behavior disabilities in leukemia patients, especially young children.

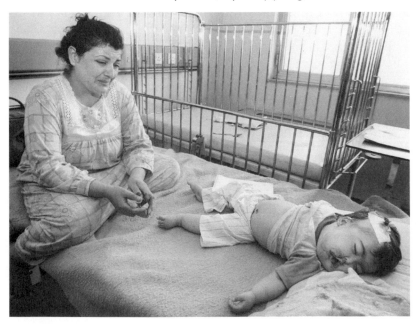

and other infections. For this reason, many children who survive leukemia do not receive vaccinations for diseases like measles, mumps, and chicken pox. This is because vaccinations give a person a mild form of the illness being vaccinated against and a child with a weakened immune system might not be able to withstand even this mild infection. They also may not be allowed to be around other children who have contagious diseases.

Bone marrow damage from treatment can also leave survivors with ongoing anemia and bleeding disorders, and lung damage from some types of chemotherapy can lead to permanent breathing difficulties; all of these conditions can prevent the individual from engaging in normal exercise and physical activities.

Another aspect of living with the aftermath of leukemia that can impact a patient's lifestyle has to do with the disruption of hormones in the body. Sometimes children who have had extensive chemotherapy and radiation must be given artificial hormones to stimulate growth and puberty later on, and young adults who wish to have children in the future often undergo a sperm or ova harvest before treatment since the drugs and radiation may destroy these cells. The sperm and ova cells may be frozen and later implanted if the individual wishes to reproduce.

A woman who is pregnant when she develops leukemia may be counseled that her own life is at risk if the pregnancy is not terminated. If this option is rejected, treatment for the leukemia must be postponed until after the baby is born, since exposure to cell-killing radiation and drugs would also kill the fetus. Either way, patients say, pregnancy, sexual functioning, and other reproductive issues are just one more aspect of living with leukemia that must be addressed.

If Treatment Fails

Sadly, many leukemia patients must deal not only with the vast array of physical, social, and emotional problems that follow treatment, but also with the reality that whatever therapy they have received is not working. In these cases, families must face the prospect of impending death, along with the need to make arrangements for end-of-life care at home, in a hospice facility, or in a traditional hospital.

In recent years a variety of public and private hospice facilities that specialize in providing guidance, comfort, and care for terminal patients and their families have opened in many locations. Some of the issues these organizations help people confront are setting new types of goals for their quality of life, attending to practical legal and financial needs, and fulfilling any hopes and dreams within reasonable reach. Brenda, for example, wanted to write a journal about certain highlights in her life before she died of CML, and her local hospice group was able to help her do this by enlisting volunteers to inscribe her memories in a bound album filled with photographs provided by family members. The experience added joy and meaning to Brenda's final days.

Some hospice and other patient support groups specialize in fulfilling the needs of terminally ill children and their families. Besides those facilities that work locally to provide care and support, there are also national and international organizations like the Make-a-Wish Foundation that are dedicated to granting final wishes for terminally ill children throughout the world. Even with the tremendous amount of sadness that accompanies the realization that death is imminent, families and medical professionals claim that such opportunities add meaning and immeasurable quality to the child's remaining time. "Wishes from the Make-a-Wish Foundation are really invaluable because they're all about enhancing the quality of life—the very life of a child threatened by certain medical conditions. Wishes have a terrific positive effect on the core of the child's spirit, his or her personality, fantasies, and dreams,"[32] says Dr. Ron Louie, chair of the board of trustees for the Make-a-Wish Foundation of Alaska, Montana, northern Idaho, and Washington.

The Make-a-Wish Foundation began in 1980 after its founders were inspired by the actions of members of the Arizona State Police, who made Chris, a seven-year-old who was dying of leukemia, an honorary police officer to fulfill his dream of someday being a policeman. The helicopter ride, uniform, and badge that Chris received brought joy into his final days, and two police officers who participated in the little boy's experience decided to make such opportunities available to other children with life-threatening illnesses. They and a group of volunteers, including Chris's mother, started the foundation to fund and arrange whatever these children wished for—whether it was a trip to Disneyland, tickets to a sports event, or sharing

Two boys from the Make-a-Wish Foundation celebrate with stock-car driver Dale Jarrett (right) after his win at the Daytona International Speedway.

a day with a favorite TV star. Soon the organization became worldwide with many local chapters, and it has since granted over eighty thousand wishes.

Similar programs like the Starlight Foundation, Grant-a-Wish, the Children's Promise Foundation, and the Sunshine Foundation have been established to fulfill the wishes of critically ill children and, in some cases, to provide hospital entertainment, assistance with housing for families of children who are hospitalized away from home, and support group services. These foundations operate through the generosity of individuals and businesses that donate money and time to make every aspect of a child's wish come true or simply to make a family's ordeal a little less stressful. Airlines, theme-park owners, hotels, celebrities, and many others donate whatever is needed to put smiles on the faces of children who may not live to see tomorrow.

Chapter 5

What the Future Holds

EVEN WITH ALL the remarkable advances in understanding and treating leukemia, the disease has not been totally conquered and is not 100 percent curable. Because the therapies available today either fail to provide lasting cures or are accompanied by terrible effects on patients, new drugs and other approaches to treatment are continuously being sought. Therefore, the Progress Review Group affiliated with the National Cancer Institute has issued a report describing research priorities that address important aspects of leukemia care and management for the present and foreseeable future. Among the more important issues they believe should be addressed in the near future are improvements in patient access to up-to-date information on the disease, along with studies on how to develop better education and training programs for specialized doctors and care centers so such facilities obtain ongoing access to the newest effective treatments.

The NCI group has also issued recommendations on necessary research into the biological and medical aspects of leukemia in order to gain more understanding of the processes by which genes, the immune system, viruses, environmental toxins, and lifestyle factors interact to cause leukemia. Such directions are already being used to promote new prevention and treatment strategies; at the present time researchers throughout the world are conducting and planning hundreds of projects they hope will improve the lives of leukemia patients and help others avoid developing the disease. Some of the most current research focuses on the following:

1. Improving drug testing, clinical trials, and patient access to promising new treatments, especially when individuals have not had good results with existing treatments.

2. Developing new drugs based on a better understanding of the genetic events and other biological processes leading up to leukemia.

3. Testing new drugs and drug combinations to establish more effective chemotherapy protocols, particularly for treatment of leukemia subtypes that are not cured by available medications.

4. Finding ways to decrease the tendency of cancer cells to become resistant to chemotherapy drugs.

5. Developing methods of bolstering a patient's immune system so it is better able to fight cancer cells.

6. Expanding research on stem cells, promoting the development of new transplant techniques, and increasing knowledge about how and why normal blood-forming stem cells turn into leukemia cells.

7. Exploring entirely new ways of treating leukemia.

Drug Testing and Clinical Trials

One important area of ongoing research involves creating and testing new and better drugs. Initially, researchers try new drugs on animals in a laboratory. Once the medication is determined to be safe and effective in animals, doctors begin clinical trials to test the substance on humans. Most clinical trials are sponsored by a research institution or a pharmaceutical company and are set up at numerous hospitals and clinics throughout the country. Patients can be referred to these studies via a personal physician's recommendation, or they can research current trials advertised by leukemia foundations or support groups and apply to be included. Rules and regulations governing such drug testing are laid out and enforced by the federal Food and Drug Administration (FDA).

Before testing a new drug on humans, doctors test the drug in animals to ensure it is safe and effective.

Three phases are involved in each clinical trial. In Phase I, a small group of patients receives the new drug to determine safe and effective doses and adverse effects. Patients who participate in clinical trials, of course, do so voluntarily with the understanding that the new treatment may or may not work for them. Many who choose this option are willing to try almost anything, however, because they have not experienced good results with standard drugs.

In Phase II, a larger group of volunteer patients is tested to insure that the experimental drug is indeed safe and produces positive results. If the drug does not appear to be helping enough people, or if it is found to have dangerous effects, the clinical trial may be halted at this point, and the drug may either be rejected as unusable or sent back to the laboratory to be refined. On the other hand, if the drug shows dramatic results and appears to be extremely safe, the FDA may waive some of the lengthy testing requirements in order to expedite widespread patient access. This can be accomplished by granting the drug a so-called fast-track status and allowing the pharmaceutical manufacturer to begin Phase III clinical testing quickly.

In Phase III, thousands of patients are enrolled in the trial and assigned either to an experimental group or a control group. Patients in the experimental group receive the new drug, while those in the control group are given an established medication currently in use as a standard leukemia treatment. In order to assess accurately whether or not the new drug is truly effective, patients are not told whether they are in the experimental or control group. This type of scientific study is known as a single-blind study. In some clinical trials, researchers go to even greater lengths to insure unbiased results by performing a double-blind study, where both patients and their doctors are not informed about which drug the patient is receiving.

Once Phase III is completed, the FDA has the authority to approve the new drug for marketing under a doctor's prescription if the medication meets FDA requirements for safety and effectiveness.

Many new drugs designed to treat and cure leukemia are currently being tested. A drug must pass through three phases of testing before the FDA approves it for marketing.

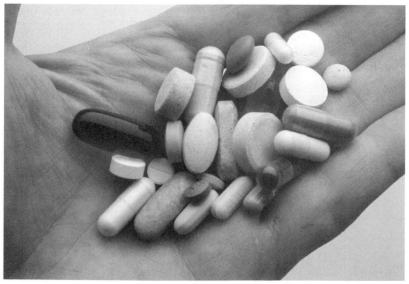

A Promising New Drug

One extremely promising new leukemia drug to which the FDA recently awarded fast-track testing status is Gleevec, also known as STI571. It is the first drug ever that was designed to target a specific part of a gene, and it works by preventing the oncogene BCR-ABL from producing leukemia cells. BCR-ABL is involved in the Philadelphia chromosome mutation found in most CML patients; thus the initial Gleevec tests were conducted on people with CML. In one of the early Phase I tests where thirty-seven CML patients received the drug, "in every single one of them, their blood counts returned to normal within one month of starting therapy, and in a significant number of them, we've actually seen the molecular cause of this leukemia begin to disappear,"[33] says one of the researchers.

Further tests have also reported a cure rate close to 100 percent, and because of these remarkable results, the FDA approved Gleevec for widespread clinical trials in record time. "This is an unprecedented drug. It promises to be one of the most effective drugs in years,"[34] states FDA acting-commissioner Dr. Bernard Schewtz.

Doctors are especially excited about Gleevec because it can be given orally, has very few unwanted effects, and does not seem to damage normal body tissues. Experts do not yet know whether the drug will be effective for long periods of time or whether it will work on other types of leukemia besides CML, but the manufacturer, Novartis, believes it may very well prove effective against other kinds of leukemia and other cancers as well. The company is moving ahead with tests to find out if this is the case.

Other New Drugs for Hard-to-Treat Subtypes

Some of the other exciting new drugs being studied seem to have the potential for successfully treating rare forms of leukemia that typically are not curable with current medications. A newly discovered substance known as bryostatin, made from small deep-sea organisms, for example, seems to halt the progression of hairy cell leukemia, a rare subtype of CLL that is very difficult to treat.

Patients with promyelocytic leukemia, a subtype of AML, also tend not to respond favorably to standard treatments but are showing good results with two new compounds. The first, a form of vitamin A known as all-trans retinoic acid, has induced remissions in 70 to 90 percent of the patients who have received it in combination with standard chemotherapy drugs. The second, arsenic trioxide, produced remissions in over 80 percent of the patients who failed to be cured with other drugs. Interestingly, scientists report that the ancient Chinese first used arsenic to treat leukemia thousands of years ago. "We confirmed the Chinese results that there's a very high incidence of complete clinical remissions in patients who are treated with low doses of arsenic trioxide with this type of leukemia,"[35] says Dr. Raymond P. Warrell Jr., a researcher at Memorial Sloan-Kettering Cancer Center in New York. Although arsenic is widely known as a deadly poison, in very small doses it can apparently trigger cancer-cell death without doing appreciable harm to normal cells.

Once used by the ancient Chinese to treat leukemia, arsenic is now a component in the new drug arsenic trioxide, which produced remissions in over 80 percent of the AML patients who failed to respond to other drugs.

Multidrug Resistance

In addition to developing new drugs and drug combinations to treat leukemia, doctors are also investigating ways of decreasing the tendency of cancer cells to become resistant to these drugs. Researchers have found that leukemia cells that have become resistant to one anticancer drug are less likely to be affected by other drugs too, a phenomenon known as multidrug resistance (MDR). They believe MDR is partly triggered by proteins called MDR pumps that bind to and expel chemotherapy agents from cancer cells. Accordingly, scientists are looking for substances that will keep these MDR pumps from operating and will therefore allow chemotherapy agents to accumulate in cancer cells. One group of researchers at Stanford University Medical Center in Palo Alto, California, for example, is testing a compound called PSC833, or valspodar, designed to bind to and disable a specific MDR pump.

A related line of research is attempting not to disable MDR pumps, but to activate them in healthy stem cells so the stem cells will not be affected by chemotherapy drugs. This could potentially be a method of protecting healthy cells from the adverse effects of cancer treatment. Doctors working on this endeavor hope someday to develop methods of inserting MDR pump genes into healthy stem cells so they will have this capability.

Other researchers addressing the MDR problem are finding that, in addition to MDR pumps, cancer cells have other ways of blocking the actions of chemotherapy drugs. In patients with B-cell lymphocytic leukemia, for instance, doctors find that certain molecules seem to protect the leukemia cells from being killed by anticancer drugs. They are therefore testing agents designed to disable these cancer-protecting molecules and make the leukemia cells more susceptible to treatment.

Immunotherapy

Since another major problem with available chemotherapy drugs is the unpleasant and dangerous effects these agents have on normal cells, other avenues of research are focusing on bolstering a

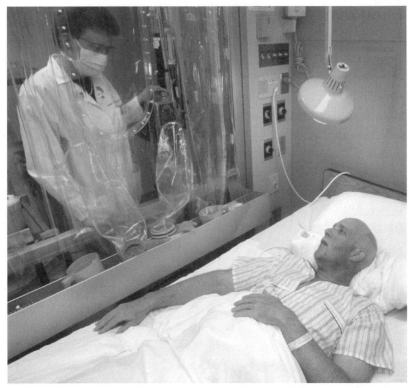

A chemotherapy patient lies in a sterile room because his immune system is weakened from treatment. New methods such as immunotherapy focus on strengthening the immune system so it can help fight leukemia cells.

patient's immune system so it can help fight leukemia cells. Such treatments, collectively known as immunotherapy, use synthetic copies of natural immune-system cells to strengthen the patient's immune system. Although some medical centers frequently administer one or more types of immunotherapy, the treatments are still considered experimental.

Antibody Treatments

One of the more promising immunotherapy techniques is called antibody treatment. This form of immunotherapy uses specially made proteins known as monoclonal antibodies to target a specific kind of cancer cell. In some cases, monoclonal antibodies are custom designed in a laboratory to attack a certain patient's cancer cells. Because of the explicit nature of their assault, these substances are sometimes dubbed smart bombs.

The proteins are called monoclonal because each molecule is engineered to be an identical clone of the other molecules. Some monoclonal antibodies are used by themselves to seek out and attack antigens in cancer cells, while others carry a radioactive agent or poison designed to kill the leukemia cells to which the antibody attaches. Both types are given intravenously.

A drug called Bexxar carries radioactive iodine and targets leukemia cells with the surface antigen whose short name is CD20. Mylotarg, a newly approved monoclonal antibody that is attached to a poison called calicheamycin, looks very promising for treating cases of adult AML that do not achieve good results with standard chemotherapy; according to the Leukemia and Lymphoma Society, "The drug is specifically for older patients who do not respond to initial treatment (refractory) or who relapse after successful initial treatment. This disease state in AML is very difficult to treat and Mylotarg has proven useful in producing or restoring remission in some patients."[36]

A very new type of treatment closely related to monoclonal antibodies is known as recombinant immunotoxin therapy. Recombinant immunotoxins are made by combining an antibody and a poison. The antibody is designed to recognize and go directly to cancer cells that have specific surface antigens, while the attached toxin's job is to destroy the cancer cell once it gets inside. NCI is now testing a recombinant immunotoxin called BL22, which appears to be giving excellent results in resistant cases of hairy cell leukemia. Dr. Ira Pastan, one of the investigators, explains:

> The preliminary results with BL22 were extremely encouraging. We expected that some patients would respond to the treatment. But we didn't imagine in our wildest dreams that almost all of the patients would go into complete remission. Half of the patients went into complete remission after a single cycle of treatment, and that was exciting to see.[37]

Immune-Cell Therapy

Another major kind of immune therapy involves injecting donor lymphocytes to try to fight leukemia cells in patients who relapse after a bone-marrow or stem-cell transplant. The rationale behind this therapy comes from the finding that after a transplant that comes from a donor rather than from the patient's own body, the transplanted immune cells often attack not only the leukemia cells, but the normal cells as well. This response is known as graft versus host disease, and it can cause dangerous infections, immune-system damage, and organ damage. Thus, researchers are investigating methods of inducing the donor lymphocytes only to go after the host's leukemia cells. At several research centers, doctors are testing a technique called graft engineering to try to add donor lymphocytes to transplanted stem cells or bone marrow in an attempt to stimulate an immune attack on the patient's leukemia cells.

Vaccines

A third line of research in immunotherapy involves developing vaccines to fight leukemia cells. "In contrast to vaccines against infectious diseases, cancer vaccines are designed to be injected after the disease is diagnosed, rather than before it develops,"[38] according to NCI.

The leukemia vaccines being studied at many research centers would ideally stimulate the patient's immune system to attack the leukemia cells. Some of these vaccines contain purified antigens taken from the person's leukemia cells and injected back into the body to trigger the immune response. Others contain cancer-cell DNA that is injected into a patient so the immune system will recognize the surface antigens as foreign and attack them.

In addition, researchers are investigating ways of fusing cancer-cell DNA with DNA from weakened cold viruses or other viruses to alert the patient's immune system that a troublesome invader is indeed present. To create this type of vaccine, first a patient's leukemia cells are collected using a leukapheresis machine. Then the leukemia cells are sent to a laboratory, where they are

Scientists at work on a cancer vaccine. Unlike other vaccines, cancer vaccines are designed to work after the disease is diagnosed, rather than before it appears.

infected with the weakened virus. The altered cells are then reinjected into the patient, whose body should be able to recognize the modified cancer-cell DNA as a foreign substance and attack it. Doctors hope the vaccine will prime the patient's immune system to continue attacking any remaining leukemia cells in the body.

Cytokines

In yet another form of immunotherapy, doctors use synthetic copies of proteins that influence the behavior of cells other than the ones from which they were produced. These proteins, called cytokines, are designed to boost a patient's immune system so it can fight leukemia cells. One type of naturally produced cytokine is interferon, which slows down cancer growth and helps stem cells mature. Interferon alpha is one synthetic substance approved by the FDA for use in treating CML in combination with chemotherapy drugs. Another cytokine, interleukin-2, stimulates the development of lymphocytes and helps them attack cancer cells. It is being tested in several studies to see if it will get a patient's lymphocytes to attack any remaining leukemia cells during a remission or after a bone-marrow transplant.

Colony-stimulating factors are additional cytokines that are being used to strengthen people's immune systems after chemotherapy or bone-marrow transplants. Colony-stimulating factors signal the bone marrow to produce healthy blood cells; there are different substances that work for different types of blood cells. These types of cytokines can also be used to draw stem cells from the bone marrow into the bloodstream so they can be harvested for a stem-cell transplant.

The cytokines show promise in improving leukemia treatment, but because they can also cause rashes, weakness, muscle and bone pain, fever, and headache, doctors are now using them primarily in patients who are at high risk of developing serious infections.

Stem-Cell Research

The use of colony-stimulating factors to facilitate stem-cell transplants and to improve a patient's resistance to infection following such a procedure is only one of the many avenues of research centering around the important blood-forming stem cells that play a role in both the causes and treatment of leukemia.

One line of research presently being explored at numerous centers, including the Fred Hutchinson Cancer Research Center in Seattle, Washington, and Harvard University in Cambridge, Massachusetts, is looking into exactly how substances known as Notch proteins signal stem cells to grow into different types of blood cells. The scientists conducting these studies also hope to discover how and why Notch proteins sometimes lose control of the signaling process, since when this happens the stem cells turn

At institutions such as the Fred Hutchinson Cancer Research Center, scientists are studying how Notch proteins lose control of the stem-signaling process, resulting in the formation of leukemia cells.

into leukemia cells. Related research at the University of Washington School of Medicine in Seattle has suggested that chromosome translocations like those in the Philadelphia chromosome may be one mechanism which disrupts Notch proteins; doctors hope eventually to use this and similar knowledge to manipulate these proteins and thereby prevent leukemia cells from forming. The researchers also anticipate that these studies will lead to new methods of growing stem cells for use in stem-cell transplants.

Another project that focuses on stem cells is being conducted at Children's Hospital of Philadelphia, where doctors are putting human stem cells containing the Philadelphia chromosome mutation into mice with defective immune systems. The researchers hope to discover how a weakened immune system helps the Philadelphia chromosome change these stem cells into leukemia cells. They also hope to identify exactly how the chromosome mutation occurs so it can possibly be prevented in the future.

Other Cutting-Edge Treatment Research

In addition to extensive new research into chemically controlling the processes by which blood-forming stem cells turn into leukemia cells, scientists have also begun studying other novel methods of treating leukemia. One such avenue of research involves developing ways of actually replacing cancer-cell DNA with normal DNA. According to the American Cancer Society:

> Greater understanding of the genes (composed of DNA) involved in certain translocations that often occur in leukemia is providing insight into why these cells may grow out of control, and why they do not develop into mature cells that participate in normal functions. Eventually, this information may be used in developing gene therapy. This treatment would replace the abnormal DNA of cancer cells with normal DNA in order to restore normal controls on cell growth.[39]

Another very new type of research concerns drugs that prevent angiogenesis, the growth of new blood vessels that nourish cancer cells. Until very recently, experts believed angiogenesis only took place with solid tumor cancers, but new evidence shows it also occurs with leukemia, where tiny new blood vessels grow in the cancerous bone marrow.

Several studies in children with leukemia found high levels of a hormone called angiogenic growth factor in the children's urine. When doctors looked at bone marrow samples with powerful microscopes, they were able to see evidence of new blood vessels growing around leukemia cells.

Researchers are currently experimenting with chemicals that disrupt this new blood-vessel growth in an attempt to starve cancer cells to death. So far, it appears that these substances, called antiangiogenic agents, also reduce the blood supply to healthy cells, so investigators are looking for ways to target only blood vessels that feed cancer cells in the hope that the drugs will someday be a potent new weapon against leukemia and other cancers.

The other cutting-edge line of research is focusing on using sensitive new techniques to detect very small numbers of leukemia

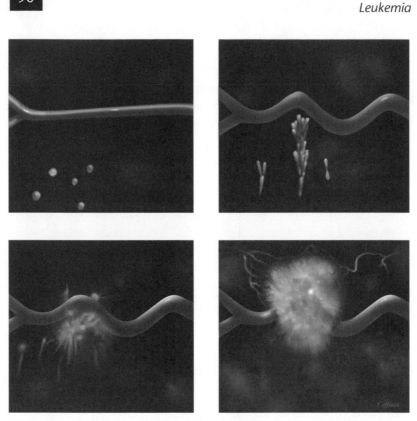

These photos show cancer cells building themselves new blood vessels. Cancer cells are experimentally injected near a blood vessel (top left); three survive to replicate and grow toward the existing blood vessel (top right); they reach the vessel (bottom left); and create new, functioning blood vessels (bottom right).

cells, even when the patient's blood and bone marrow appear to be leukemia-free when viewed under a microscope. This type of research is known as detection of minimal residual disease, and doctors hope it will help achieve more permanent leukemia cures by accurately assessing remissions. Researchers at St. Jude Hospital in Memphis, Tennessee, for example, are using these tests to detect as little as one leukemia cell per ten thousand normal cells and have discovered that nearly one-quarter of the patients they believed were in remission actually had minimal residual disease. Since any remaining leukemia cells are associated with a higher risk of relapse, the researchers are continuing to give patients with any cancer cells chemotherapy until all these cells are gone.

Conclusion

With all the recent progress in understanding the molecular causes, developing new treatments, and monitoring leukemia patients' conditions after remission, experts believe the cure rates for all types of leukemia will increase in the near future. The battle against leukemia advances slowly toward the time when this dreaded cancer will yield to reliable, easily tolerated, inexpensive treatments and thus cease to inspire fear and suffering whenever it strikes.

Notes

Introduction: A Dreaded and Frightening Disease

1. Quoted in Leukemia and Lymphoma Society, "Toby." www.leukemia-lymphoma.org/all_soh_detail.adp?item_id=33359&cat_id=1157.

2. S.K. Kaura, *A Family Doctor's Guide to Understanding and Preventing Cancer*. Santa Fe, NM: Health Press, 1991, p. xv.

3. Quoted in Leukemia and Lymphoma Society, "Marquita." www.leukemia-lymphoma.org/all_soh_detail.adp?item_id=33346&cat_id=1157.

4. Jim Atkinson, "Playing for Keeps," *Texas Monthly*, July 1999, p. 52.

Chapter 1: What Is Leukemia?

5. Leukemia & Lymphoma Society, "Chronic Lymphocytic Leukemia (CLL)." www.leukemia-lymphoma.org/all_mat_detail.adp?item_id=3221&sort_order=7&cat_id=.

6. Barbara Lackritz, *Adult Leukemia*. Sebastopol, CA: O'Reilly and Associates, 2001, p. 24.

7. Quoted in Grant Steen and Joseph Mirro, eds., *Childhood Cancer*. Cambridge, MA: Perseus, 2000, p. 316.

Chapter 2: What Causes Leukemia?

8. Quoted in Atkinson, "Playing for Keeps," p. 52.

9. American Cancer Society, "Can Leukemia Be Prevented?" http://cancer.org/eprise/main/docroot/CRI/content.

10. American Cancer Society, "History of Cancer." www3.cancer.

org/cancerinfo/load_cont.asp?ct=1.

11. Quoted in National Institute of Environmental Health Sciences, "Environmental Health Institute Report Concludes Evidence Is 'Weak' That EMF's Cause Cancer." www.niehs. nih.gov/oc/news/emffin.htm.

12. American Cancer Society, "What Causes Acute Leukemia? Can It Be Prevented?" www.cancer.org/eprise/main/docroot/ CRI/content.

13. Dan Kennedy, "Toxic Trial," *Boston Phoenix*, August 18, 1995.

14. Leukemia and Lymphoma Society, "Facts and Statistics." www.leukemia-lymphoma.org/all_page?item_id=12486.

15. University of California, San Francisco, "Common Genetic Differences Affect Vulnerability to Leukemia." http://pub. ucsf.edu/today/news.php?news_id=200103263.

Chapter 3: Leukemia Treatment

16. Quoted in Jewish Women's Archive, "Gertrude Elion." www.jwa.org/exhibits/elion/research.htm.

17. National Academy of Science, "Curing Childhood Leukemia." www4.nas.edu/beyond/beyonddiscovery.nsf/ web/leukemia7.

18. National Academy of Science, "Curing Childhood Leukemia." www4.nas.edu/beyond/beyonddiscovery.nsf/ web/leukemia8.

19. National Cancer Institute, "Treatment." http://cancernet. nci.nih.gov/wyntk_pubs/leukemia.htm.

20. Quoted in Leukemia and Lymphoma Society, "Annette," p. 2. www.leukemia-lymphoma.org/all_soh_detail.adp? itemid=8843&cat_id=1157.

21. Baruch Margalit, interview by author, San Luis Obispo, CA, August 29, 2001.

22. Quoted in Arthur L. Jones, "Lifeline: Solitary Confinement; One Man's Battle Against Cancer Forces Him to Face a Per-

sonal Demon: His Hospital Room," *Washington Post*, March 28, 2000, p. Z10.

Chapter 4: Living with Leukemia

23. Quoted in Steen and Mirro, *Childhood Cancer*, p. 569.

24. Quoted in Steen and Mirro, *Childhood Cancer*, p. 552.

25. Margalit, interview.

26. Quoted in Leukemia and Lymphoma Society, "Marquita."

27. Quoted in Steen and Mirro, *Childhood Cancer*, p. 464.

28. Quoted in Lackritz, *Adult Leukemia*, p. 49.

29. Quoted in Leukemia and Lymphoma Society, "Annette," p. 2.

30. Lackritz, *Adult Leukemia*, p. 357.

31. Quoted in Lackritz, *Adult Leukemia*, p. 182.

32. Quoted in Make-a-Wish Foundation, "The Voice of a Medical Professional." www.wish.org/home/frame_aboutus.htm.

Chapter 5: What the Future Holds

33. Quoted in CNN.com, "Drug Shows Promise Against One Form of Leukemia," p.1. www.cnn.com/1999/HEALTH/12/03/leukemia.pill.02.

34. Quoted in Leukemia and Lymphoma Society, "FDA Approves Leukemia Drug in Record Time," p. 1. www.leukemia-lymphoma.org/all_news_detail?news_type=1&source_id=5&item_id=19000&cat_id=1.

35. Quoted in CNN Interactive, "Study: Arsenic Found Successful in Treating Leukemia," p. 1. www.cnn.com/HEALTH/9811/07/arsenic.leukemia.

36. Leukemia and Lymphoma Society, "Monoclonal Antibodies: Applied in the Treatment of Acute Myelogenous Leukemia (AML)," p. 2. www.leukemia-lymphoma.org/all_news_detail?news_type=1&source_id=4&item_id=13782&cat_id=1.

37. "Scientists Report Complete Remissions in Early Leukemia Trial," *News from the NCI*, July 25, 2001, p. 1.

38. National Cancer Institute, "Biological Therapies: Using the Immune System to Treat Cancer." http://cis.nci.nih.gov/fact/7_2.htm.

39. American Cancer Society, "What's New in Leukemia Research and Treatment?" www.cancer.org/eprise/main/docroot/CRI/content.

Glossary

allogeneic transplant: A transplant where another person donates tissue.

anemia: A condition caused by too few red blood cells.

angiogenesis: The growth of new blood vessels that nourish cancer cells.

antibody: A protein produced by the immune system to fight an invading antigen.

antigen: A protein in an invading cell that triggers an immune response by a living creature.

autologous transplant: A transplant where the patient donates his or her own tissue.

biopsy: Removal of a sample of tissue for laboratory study.

blast: An immature, nonfunctional, cancerous white blood cell.

blood-forming stem cell: A cell in the bone marrow from which all blood cells grow.

bone marrow: Soft tissue inside bone cavities where blood cells are formed.

chemotherapy: Treatment consisting of the administration of one or more anticancer drugs.

chromosome: One of the forty-six wormlike structures in a human cell nucleus that contains genetic material.

clinical trial: A research study that tests a new medical treatment on patients.

cytokines: Proteins produced by one cell that influence another cell.

gene: The part of a DNA molecule that transmits hereditary information.

granulocyte: A type of white blood cell that matures in the bone marrow.

hematologist: A physician who specializes in diagnosing and treating blood disorders.

immunotherapy: The use of synthetic immune cells to fight a disease.

leukapheresis: A technique for removing excess white blood cells from the bloodstream.

leukemia: A cancer characterized by uncontrolled growth of white blood cells.

leukocytes: White blood cells.

lymphocytes: White blood cells that mature in the lymph system.

lymphocytic leukemias: Leukemias that affect white blood cells known as lymphocytes.

malignant: Cancerous.

monoclonal antibody: An antibody made in the laboratory that is able to attack specific cancer cells.

monocyte: A type of white blood cell that matures in the bone marrow.

mutation: A change in a gene that can alter a cell's functioning.

myelogenous leukemias: Leukemias that affect white blood cells that mature in the bone marrow.

oncogene: A cancer-causing gene.

oncologist: A physician who specializes in diagnosing and treating cancer.

platelets: Colorless blood cells that repair blood vessels by beginning the clotting process.

relapse: A return of a disease after its apparent disappearance.

remission: A decrease or disappearance of disease signs and symptoms.

transfusion: Putting blood into a patient's veins from an outside source.

translocaton: A chromosome abnormality that occurs when a piece of one chromosome breaks off and attaches to another chromosome.

Organizations to Contact

American Cancer Society
Addresses are given in local phone directories.
(800) ACS-2345
website: www3.cancer.org

The American Cancer Society provides information on prevention, causes, diagnosis, research, treatment, and living with cancer.

Leukemia and Lymphoma Society
1311 Mamaroneck Ave.
White Plains, NY 10605
(800) 955-4572
website: www.leukemia-lymphoma.org

The Leukemia and Lymphoma Society provides information on all aspects of leukemia, including diagnosis, treatment, research, and support services. Free pamphlets are available on disease information and living strategies.

Leukemia Research Foundation
820 Davis St., Suite 420
Evanston, IL 60201
(847) 424-0600
website: www.leukemiaresearch.org

The Leukemia Research Foundation furnishes information on research, coping skills, and quality-of-life resources.

National Cancer Institute
Public Inquiries Office
Bldg. 31, Room 10A31, 31 Center Dr., MSC 2580
Bethesda, MD 20892
(301) 435-3848 or (800) 422-6237
website: www.nci.nih.gov

The National Cancer Institute provides information on all types of cancer, including leukemia. The information covers research, support services, clinical trials, and basic disease information. Free booklets are available covering research, treatment, and living with the disease.

For Further Reading

Books

Melanie A. Apel, *Coping with Leukemia*. New York: Rosen, 2000. Talks about diagnosis, treatment, and coping; written especially for teens whose lives have been touched by leukemia.

Nancy Keene, *Childhood Leukemia: A Guide for Families, Friends, and Caregivers*. Sebastopol, CA: O'Reilly and Associates, 1999. Offers an easy-to-read explanation of the disease, including symptoms, diagnosis, treatment, and practical living and coping strategies.

John Lazlo, *The Cure of Childhood Leukemia: Into the Age of Miracles*. New Brunswick, NJ: Rutgers University Press, 1995. Dr. Lazlo tells the story of the remarkable transformation of childhood leukemia from inevitably fatal to usually curable.

Internet Source

National Academy of Science, "Curing Childhood Leukemia." www4.nas.edu/beyond/beyonddiscovery.nsf/web/leukemia. Detailed account of the events leading up to the discovery of a cure for childhood leukemia.

Website

Granny Barb and Art's Leukemia Links (www.acor.org/leukemia). Part of the Association of Cancer Online Resources, provides diverse information and support links.

Works Consulted

Books

S. K. Kaura, *A Family Doctor's Guide to Understanding and Preventing Cancer.* Santa Fe, NM: Health Press, 1991. Readable overview of cancer in general.

Barbara Lackritz, *Adult Leukemia.* Sebastopol, CA: O'Reilly and Associates, 2001. Informative guide written by a leukemia survivor and patient advocate. Covers all issues relating to the disease and support services.

Leif E. Peterson and Seymour Abrahamson, eds., *Effects of Ionizing Radiation.* Washington, DC: Joseph Henry Press, 1998. Detailed and highly technical studies on the effects of radiation exposure from atomic bombs.

Grant Steen and Joseph Mirro, eds., *Childhood Cancer.* Cambridge, MA: Perseus, 2000. Covers all childhood cancers with two chapters on childhood leukemias; other easily understood chapters on gene mutations and coping issues.

Marcella Liffick Stevens, *Fundamentals of Clinical Hematology.* Philadelphia: W.B. Saunders, 1997. Medical-school textbook covering blood physiology and diseases.

Periodicals

Jim Atkinson, "Playing for Keeps," *Texas Monthly,* July 1999.

"Gauging the Risk of Leukemia Relapse," *St. Jude Rounds,* Fall 1999.

Arthur L. Jones, "Lifeline: Solitary Confinement; One Man's

Battle Against Cancer Forces Him to Face a Personal Demon: His Hospital Room," *Washington Post*, March 28, 2000.

Dan Kennedy, "Toxic Trial," *Boston Phoenix*, August 18, 1995.

H. Li, et al., "The Presence of Ancient Human T-Cell Lymphotropic Virus Type 1 Provirus DNA in an Andean Mummy," *Nature Medicine 5*, December 1999.

Christine Many, "Saved by Her Sister," *Ladies Home Journal*, May 2000.

B.M. Rothschild, et al., "Recognition of Leukemia in Skeletal Remains: Report and Comparison of Two Cases," *American Journal of Physical Anthropology*, 1997.

"Scientists Report Complete Remissions in Early Leukemia Trial," *News from the NCI*, July 25, 2001.

Kim Tolnair and Esther Crain, "I Came Back from Death to Be a Cancer Crusader," *Cosmopolitan*, January 1999.

Internet Sources

American Cancer Society, "Can Leukemia Be Prevented?" http://cancer.org/eprise/main/docroot/CRI/content.

———, "History of Cancer." www3.cancer.org/cancerinfo/load_cont.asp?ct=1.

———, "What Causes Acute Leukemia? Can It Be Prevented?" www.cancer.org/eprise/main/docroot/CRI/content.

———, "What's New in Leukemia Research and Treatment?" www.cancer.org/eprise/main/docroot/CRI/content.

CNN.com, "Drug Shows Promise Against One Form of Leukemia." www.cnn.com/1999/HEALTH/12/03/leukemia.pill.02.

CNN Interactive, "Study: Arsenic Found Successful in Treating Leukemia." www.cnn.com/HEALTH/9811/07/arsenic.leukemia.

Jewish Women's Archive, "Gertrude Elion." www.jwa.org/exhibits/elion/research.htm.

Leukemia and Lymphoma Society, "Acute Lymphocytic Leukemia (ALL)." www.leukemia-lymphoma.org/all_mat_ detail.adp?item_id=248&sort_order=16&cat_id=.

———, "Acute Myelogenous Leukemia (AML)." www. leukemia-lymphoma.org/all_mat_detail.adp?item_id=3313& sort_order=4&cat_id=.

———, "Annette." www.leukemia-lymphoma.org/all_soh_detail. adp?item_id=8843&cat_id=1157.

———, "Chemotherapy." www.leukemia-lymphoma.org/all_ page?item_id=8498.

———, "Chronic Lymphocytic Leukemia (CLL)." www. leukemia-lymphoma.org/all_mat_detail.adp?item_id=3221& sort_order=4&cat_id=.

———, "Chronic Myelogenous Leukemia (CML)." www. leukemia-lymphoma.org/all_mat_detail.adp? item_id=2119&sort_order=7&cat_id=.

———, "Clinical Trials." www.leukemia-lymphoma.org/all_ page?item_id=8492.

———, "Complementary Therapy." www.leukemia-lymphoma. org/all_page?item_id=8495.

———, "Facts and Statistics." www.leukemia-lymphoma.org/ all_page?item_id=12486.

———, "FDA Approves Alemtuzumab for Refractory Chronic Lymphocytic Leukemia." www.leukemia-lymphoma.org/all_ news_detail?news_type=1&source_id=6&item_id=20367&cat_ id=1.

———, "FDA Approves Leukemia Drug in Record Time." www.leukemia-lymphoma.org/all_news_detail? news_type=1&source_id=5&item_id=19000&cat_id=1.

———, "Leukemia." www.leukemia-lymphoma.org/all_page? item_id=9346.

————, "Marquita." www.leukemia-lymphoma.org/all_soh_detail. adp?item_id=33346&cat_id=1157.

————, "Monoclonal Antibodies: Applied in the Treatment of Acute Myelogenous Leukemia (AML)." www.leukemia-lymphoma. org/all_news_detail?news_type=1&source_id=4&item_id=1378 2&cat_id=1.

————, "Novel Agent Shows Anti-Leukemic Activity." www.leukemia-lymphoma.org/all_news_detail? news_type=1&source_id=6&item_id=9055&cat_id=1.

————, "Radiation Therapy." www.leukemia-lymphoma.org/ all_page?item_id=9083.

————, "Stem Cell Transplant." www.leukemia-lymphoma.org/ all_page?item_id=5965.

————, "Toby." www.leukemia-lymphoma.org/all_soh_detail. adp?item_id=33359&cat_id=1157.

Make-a-Wish Foundation, "The Voice of a Medical Professional." www.wish.org/home/frame_aboutus.htm.

National Academy of Science, "Curing Childhood Leukemia." www4.nas.edu/beyond/beyonddiscovery.nsf/web/leukemia.

National Cancer Institute, "Biological Therapies: Using the Immune System to Treat Cancer." http://cis.nci.nih.gov/fact/ 7_2.htm.

————, "Report of the Leukemia, Lymphoma, and Myeloma Progress Review Group," May 2001. http://osp.nci.nih. gov/Prg_assess/PRG/LLMPRO/llm_rpt.htm.

————, "Treatment." http://cancernet.nci.nih.gov/wyntk_ pubs/leukemia.htm.

National Institute of Environmental Health Sciences, "Benzene." http://ehis.niehs.nih.gov/roc/ninth/known/benzene.pdf.

————, "Environmental Health Institute Report Concludes Evidence Is 'Weak' That EMF's Cause Cancer." www.niehs.nih. gov/oc/news/emffin.htm.

Kristine Novak, "Secret of the Mummies' Tomb," *Nature Science Update,* November 30, 1999. www.nature.com/nsu/991202/991202-5.html.

United States Department of Energy, "Chernobyl Health Effects Studies." http://tis.ch.doe.gov/ihp/jccc/chernobyl.html.

University of California, San Francisco, "Common Genetic Differences Affect Vulnerability to Leukemia." http://pub.ucsf.edu/today/news.php?news_id=200103263.

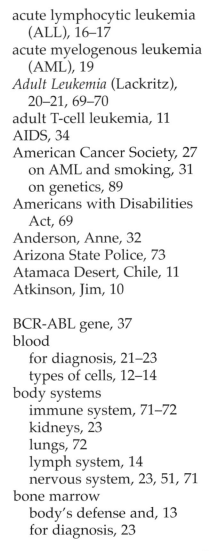

Index

Picture Credits

Cover Photo: © Cindy Karp/Black Star Publishing/PictureQuest
© AFP/CORBIS, 68, 71, 88
American Cancer Society, 66
© Lester V. Bergman/CORBIS, 12, 15, 18, 81
© Bettmann/CORBIS, 9, 29, 42, 45
© Bohemian Nomad Picturemakers/CORBIS, 57
© Laura Dwight/CORBIS, 39
Chris Jouan, 21
© Larry Mulvehill/Photo Researchers, 53
© Richard T. Nowitz/CORBIS, 55
PhotoDisc, 22, 24, 31, 35, 36, 78, 79
Photofest, 33
© Roger Ressmeyer/CORBIS, 62, 86
© Reuters NewMedia Inc./CORBIS, 74, 90
© Leif Skoogfors/CORBIS, 47, 83
© David and Peter Turnley/CORBIS, 60, 65
© David H. Wells/CORBIS, 50

About the Author

Melissa Abramovitz has been writing books, articles, poetry, and short stories as a freelance writer for children, teenagers, and adults for over fifteen years. During this time she has published hundreds of nonfiction articles, numerous short stories and poems, one novel, and five educational children's books.

The author grew up in San Diego, California, and developed an interest in medical topics as a teenager. At one time she thought she wanted to become a doctor, but she ended up getting her degree in psychology from the University of California, San Diego, in 1976. She currently lives in San Luis Obispo, California, with her husband, two teenaged sons, and two extremely spoiled dogs.